CW00566057

A
WOODMAN'S
LOT

A WOODMAN'S LOT

BY MICHAEL BOXALL

BROWN
DOG
BOOKS

Copyright © Michael Boxall 2014

The right of Michael Boxall to be identified as the author of this work has been asserted in accordance with the Copyright, Designs & Patents Act 1988.

All rights reserved. No part of this book may be reproduced, stored in a retrieval system, or transmitted in any form or by any means, electronic, electrostatic, magnetic tape, mechanical, photocopying, recording or otherwise, without the written permission of the copyright holder.

Published under licence by Brown Dog Books and
The Self Publishing Partnership
7 Green Park Station, Bath BA1 1JB

www.selfpublishingpartnership.co.uk

ISBN printed book: 978-1-78545-001-3
ISBN e-book: 978-1-78545-002-0

Cover design by Andrew Easton

Printed and bound by CPI Group (UK) Ltd, Croydon CR0 4YY

INTRODUCTION

West Dean Estate extends across 6,000 acres of the South Downs in West Sussex around the village, which is unusual in that it has no council houses: a few properties had been sold off over the years and a small number of social houses built, but it remains overwhelmingly the estate's village. In the 1890s, when bought by William James, the estate had been considerably larger, but as is the way of the world, woods and farmland around the periphery were subsequently sold. When William James died it was inherited by his eccentric art connoisseur son, Edward, who, to ensure its continuance after his death, oversaw its transition into the Edward James Foundation administered by a board of trustees. The big house, which for years had been a private girl's school was developed into West Dean College and now has an international reputation for teaching the finest quality art and craft courses. The estate itself consists of a mixture of tenanted and in-hand farms, an arboretum and two thousand acres of woodland.

I was born in 7 The Warren, one of a terrace of four brick built cottages at the western edge of the village on the fifth of November 1947 and am eternally grateful my parents resisted a request from Alfred, my great grandfather, that I be christened Guy. My first ten years were spent in the village and I attended the primary school, though we moved two miles south to the much larger village of Lavant in 1957, where one of my sisters still lives. Secondary school in Chichester and my first job as an apprentice engineer at N. Tamplin and Co Ltd on the Birdham straight south of the city cut my ties with West Dean, though I still visited my grandparents at number 7. I learned a great deal during my days at Tamplins including welding and lathe work, but the prospect of eventually becoming their chief buyer with a desk, telephone, company car and secretary, no matter how attractive held not the slightest appeal: I harboured a growing desire to work with nature, not steel. In 1968 I became a Voluntary warden with the Nature Conservancy (after several metamorphoses now titled Natural England) at Kingley Vale National Nature Reserve and the thought of being employed to do what I enjoyed most was my idea of heaven. I put in countless hours of unpaid labour to help the warden, Richard Williamson, read all I could find about conservation and applied for numerous jobs with organisations large and small, from Cornwall to Dumfries and Galloway. I wrote to Nature Conservancy headquarters asking how I could increase my chance of success in their periodic 'competitions', when warden's posts were advertised and they suggested estate management or forestry: I chose the latter and cheerfully bid steel fabrication farewell. Though I reached their reserve list more than once, the goal continued to elude me and for many reasons I am very glad things turned out differently, not least that my choice meant a return to West Dean, for there was a vacancy in the Woods Department.

Through the thirteen and a half years I worked in the woods there was a slow turnover of staff due to retirements, the much greater sadness of deaths and a trickle for whom a period of practical experience was required before they went on to college with the intention of becoming qualified foresters. There were also a few who fancied the freedom of an outdoor life, until they came face to face with its sometimes harsh and very physical realities: they didn't stay long. This is why names will come and go throughout the book and rarely have arrival or departure dates been mentioned in any detail in order to keep focused on the subject; my small part in what is already history. I have not changed any names and everything related actually happened: there are no 'fisherman's tales', though occasionally events from more than one year have been combined in a chapter to provide a more rounded picture of the activity described. I hope, should those who shared these years with me and have not passed on to that far greater forest read the book, that it will bring back memories of their own time in the woods; the wet, cold, heat, great physical exertions and rough sense of humour we shared and enjoyed, sometimes endured, together. I thank them all for helping to make this period a very special part of my life.

Glossary of Forestry Terms used in the Book

(Some of these are very local, others are used nationwide)

Bearer – A length of wood on which other wood is stacked, or to bridge a gap over which timber is to be rolled.

Bender – A small tree or sapling pulled over and held down under great tension, usually by another, larger tree which has fallen or been felled.

Break – A point where the diameter of a tree changes significantly, causing it to be measured as two or more separate lengths.

Butt – The trunk of a tree and the name given to six foot lengths of conifer to be used for making panel fencing.

Butt end – The bottom, cut end of a felled tree

Cant – A number of rows of trees in a plantation worked by an individual sawyer during thinning.

Canthook – A curved steel hook attached to the side of a long wooden handle and used for turning heavy logs.

Claws – The top of a tree's roots where they join the trunk.

Coppice – The regrowth from the stump of a cut tree or bush, usually referring to hazel or sweet chestnut, species which have been managed in this way for millennia to provide rods and poles.

Cube – One hoppus foot, the unit of measurement for round timber, containing a cubic foot.

Cuckoo – A tree lodged against another as a result of felling or windblow.

Dogs – Fencing pliers.

Faghook – A tool like a sickle, but with a cranked handle making it right or left handed.

Handbill – Also called a billhook. A one-handed tool used for cutting small rods, marking trees for felling and other jobs.

Head off – To cut off the top of a felled tree at a point where its diameter becomes too small to produce any further useful wood.

Heel in – To temporarily store young trees in the ground, usually in bundles, to keep their roots moist until they are required for planting.

Hoppus tables – A book of calculated timber volumes under length and diameter: these are used in conjunction with a girth tape to find the volume of a butt.

Lot – A quantity of standing timber offered for sale.

Maiden – A tree naturally regenerated from seed.

Maul – A heavy, long handled hammer with a head shaped like a cotton reel: used for hammering in stakes. Not to be used for striking metal as the head could shatter.

Moor – The upturned rootplate of a windblown tree.

Parcel – A quantity of felled timber.

Rack – An access created in young plantations by the felling of a row of trees.

Shake – Cracks in the timber of growing trees, usually oak or sweet **chestnut** - ring shake occurs along the annual growth rings and star shake from the central pith: if severe it can render a butt useless for anything except firewood.

Singling – Cutting all but one stem from a multi-stemmed tree to produce future timber.

Sink – The wedge shaped piece cut out to aim a tree during felling.

Skeg – The sharp stub of a broken or sawn off branch

Slasher – A long handled sickle.

Sling – A steel cable like the winch rope but with eyes at both ends; used to give extra reach when winching.

Trim out – The cutting away of all branches from a felled tree.

Weeding – Trimming around young trees to give their leading shoots light and space.

Widowmaker – A broken branch or hung up tree which could fall without warning.

Winch rope – the steel cable on the winch drum.

CHAPTER 1
A HOT WELCOME

Seven o'clock on July 6th 1970, a morning of thick mist saw me entering the yard for the first time. A small knot of men were gathered beneath an open fronted shed, half of which was filled by a mud encrusted long wheelbase Land-Rover. In thick dust covering its rear door a finger had scrawled "Jack's roller coaster 6d a ride". Beside the shed stood a diesel tank: painted with red oxide when new, it was stained with rust, dust and spilled fuel, its side emblazoned DERV in peeling black letters – diesel engined road vehicle – in front of which an unknown hand had printed HORS with a piece of chalk. They were evidently cultured woodmen. Chris, my playmate of primary school days greeted me: we had both attended the village school and our ages differed only by a few months. Others I recognised by sight and my family was well known to most, so the butterflies in my stomach didn't flutter as violently as they would otherwise have done. Someone produced a quantity of slashers and cigar stones from the tool store, laying them in the vehicle with a loud clatter: it was the signal to climb aboard. As new boy I had the dubious honour of being last in, expected to pull the door shut on the crush of bodies, lunchbags and steel toecapped boots seeking space among the slashers: the industry that is now health and safety thankfully unheard of in those days. It soon dawned on me there was a hierarchy in this apparent chaos: the most experienced sat forward with me, the lowliest recruit relegated to the back where I had the benefit of windows but the most uncomfortable position. Only Jack and Snowy who sat in the front had padded seats: the rest of us had to make do with the bare aluminium wheel arches. Our destination they told me was Blackbush plantation, at the northern end of Bow Hill.

The Land-Rover bowled along, engine humming and gearbox emitting the lovely whine characteristic of the breed in those less refined days, the interior filled with smoke and conversation. I don't smoke and said little, but watched through the dusty windows the lane trailing in our wake, hedges on either side heavy with summer foliage, leaves rustling soundlessly in the wind of our passing before they were swallowed by the grey mist. When we came to the chalky track ascending Bow Hill I discovered the words on the rear door were more than mere graffiti: the vehicle bucked and rolled in and out of the sun hardened ruts like a ship beating into a heavy sea. Sitting behind the rear wheels meant I was catapulted off my seat several times, returning with thumps of varying intensity. The swaying and rolling became worse as we drove along the track through the centre of the plantation then ceased abruptly with a slight squeak of brakes. There were a few moments of silence when the engine stopped before everyone piled out to begin the day's work, cutting back vegetation along rows of young trees: they had started the previous week and half the plantation had already been 'weeded'.

Jack, the assistant forester, led the gang and Snowy usually drove the Land-Rover: he was foreman and under the circumstances I thought should have had his name on the rear door. He handed me a slasher and sharpening stone, assigned me a row and explained that it was necessary to trim back anything interfering with the leading shoot of each tree. They had been planted at six feet spacing with six feet between each row, a mixture of beech and larch. "Try not to cut any off," he said before starting to sharpen his slasher. I did likewise, resting the end of the handle against my instep and the blade flat against the palm of my right hand so I could use the stone on it without my fingers getting in the way. It didn't need much rubbing to give the thin steel a keen edge and I was soon ready to go. Looking for my row, I could see the first tree, a fine little beech clearly visible amid the paler green of sun dried summer grasses and a few flicks of the blade were sufficient to free its top. Next in line was a larch, struggling up amid a low gorse bush: this required heavier and more deliberate work, threading the blade between the spiny fingers and all important leading shoot before pulling it up and outwards as hard and quickly as I could. Two done and the third visible; I could now be sure of the line and began slashing away merrily, the third and fourth trees needing little attention. Then the inevitable happened: a misdirected swipe topped a promising larch. As I was already lagging behind no-one noticed, but feeling guilty and foolish I stood the severed head upright just in case and resolved to take greater care from then on.

What had begun as a fairly clear row now vanished among gorse and thorn more than waist high, with bramble threaded through the bushes for good measure: this slowed my progress considerably as the small trees proved very difficult to see beneath the tangle. The gap between myself and the rest of the gang was widening at almost every step and there was no way I could put on a spurt to catch up. The bushes fought back as I hacked and swung at them, stabbing my legs, a bramble dragging across my knee leaving several stout hooked prickles embedded in jeans and the flesh beneath: at least my boots kept them at bay. My temperature rose and sweat began to flow liberally. With a loud thud the blade struck a hidden stump, jarring my hands and embedding itself so firmly I had to rock it back and forth several times to ease it free. The mist burned away before I was halfway along the row and the sun beamed down from a cloudless sky, preparing the still air for what was to come, a temperature of 90 degrees by early afternoon. The wet grass, which had rapidly soaked my boots and the bottom of my jeans when we started dried out almost as I looked at it, droplets of sapphire, emerald and ruby left by the mist sparkled briefly in the sunlight before his warmth steamed them into invisibility. On and on, trimming gently here, forcefully there; more thorns, more scratches and a great deal more sweat: at least the trees were easy to locate and there were no further mishaps. The fastest workers reached the end of their rows long before me, leaning against the rabbit proof netting fence which surrounded the plantation to sharpen their slashers and take a breather. I struggled on, my shirt already damp with sweat and reached the last tree as they began the return rows. There was time only for a brief touch-up of the now very dull blade before I followed on, ominous warmth becoming apparent at the base of one finger on my left hand. Soon I was lagging again and unable, no matter how hard I tried, to catch up.

More gorse to plough through and with it appeared the detached top of a beech: I saw it only as it somersaulted accusingly in the air. Treading it quickly into the spiky green mass I continued, thankful once more that the crime had not been witnessed. The heat in my finger was becoming painful, that in my face producing rivers of sweat and the temperature was rising rapidly. Through the gorse with a few more swipes, at last several trees showed across a grassy area. I made only a token effort here because they were in no danger of being overgrown and tackled the thorns which next impeded progress: it seemed a very long way across the hillside to the central ride, the Land-Rover and my lunchbag. More gorse, more thorns and some welcome patches of grass where only the lightest flick of the blade was needed: I was wilting already and there could be no respite until we reached the vehicle. The blade had quickly become very dull again, which made cutting harder work and slowed me down even more: there was no choice but to stop and sharpen it. The distance between me and the next man was now almost thirty yards and likely to be even greater by the time he reached the ride. Having restored the cutting edge I knocked the stone against the side of the blade to clear it of carborundum dust and slid it into a back pocket before bending once more to the task. Heat waves were already shimmering across the plantation and a swarm of flies buzzed incessantly round my head, though I paid the sound little heed as rarely did one try to settle while I kept moving. Jack reached the ride first and stood for a moment watching the others, as one by one they joined him. It was with immense relief I saw Snowy, instead of starting his break, turn round and begin working back along my row, saving me several yards of effort.

We sat down along the ride edge, for it was too hot to be crammed into the vehicle. I leaned back gratefully against a sturdy young oak and opened my bag: not knowing what to expect I had brought my sandwich box, but only a quart flask of tea which I could happily have quaffed in one go. Rationing myself to a single cup I sipped it slowly, savouring every drop. A sandwich felt dry as dust in my already parched mouth, but I needed the energy it contained. The oak provided welcome shade from the hot sun, though I continued to sweat: my arms were already tired and the heat in my finger had resolved itself into a large, pale blister. Laying back against the rough bark was sheer bliss and I knew, too good to last long. The dreaded moment came: Jack stood up and said "C'mon some o' these, before it gets hot." As understatements go it would take some beating; it was already hot, very hot, the temperature increasing by the minute.

Reluctantly I got to my feet and picked up the slasher, giving it a good sharp-up before setting into my next row. Within minutes I was lagging behind once more and the restorative effects of our short break had been used up. The blister became so painful I could no longer grip the handle with that finger and was forced to hold more firmly with the rest, a recipe for disaster. All too soon another began forming and the first burst. A whippy gorse bush drew blood as it stabbed into my knuckles and the resulting spots of liquid red drew away some of the flies circling endlessly round my head. The sun beat down with increasing intensity and I felt like a man lost in the Sahara, the oasis of my flask beyond reach until we stopped for dinner. I was working now like an automaton, intent only on keeping up as well as I could, trying hard not to think how long it was before I could have another drink. Swing, swing, swipe; the action felt as if it had been going on forever and would continue ever more.

A horsefly bit David between the shoulder blades, causing him to leap in the air with an exaggerated cry of pain. Laughter rolled across the plantation and there were several offers of help to squash the offending insect with a slasher. I may have gained a little ground as the merriment caused a momentary halt to progress, but was unable to maintain the advance. A slasher is not a heavy tool, but mine now felt as though it weighed a ton as I swung it back and forth, my arms telling me they were lengthening in direct proportion to the increasing weight, and I longed for a few moments respite. Jack continued to forge steadily on, to all appearances fresh as a daisy, little Snowy also, but the younger members of the gang seemed to be showing signs of being affected by the heat. This was a great relief: it didn't mean I could catch them up because I was undoubtedly more tired than they were, but there was the happy possibility of getting no further behind provided I continued as fast as possible.

I inflicted one more case of 'Sheffield Blight', as cutting the top off these little trees was known, before reaching the end of my row, unaided this time. Praise be! The deep shade of an old yew beckoned and no-one had started back along new rows: the tremendous heat was obviously telling. I leaned back against the fence dripping with sweat: the second blister had burst but no longer was there much obvious pain. The wetness helped maintain a firm grip on the handle and was certainly not an impediment to sharpening. "Three more rows then we'll have dinner," said Jack finally: this was depressing news as it meant a further two hours before liquid could pass my lips! I had only been stopped a couple of minutes yet every muscle protested almost audibly at being asked to resume activity. My legs were scratched from top to bottom through the inadequate protection of Levi's best denim; both hands were speckled with dried blood and my face felt as though it was on fire, roasting from a combination of sunburn and internal heat. I wanted to take my shirt off but knew that would be foolish as my fair skin would burn to a crisp in no time, so settled for undoing all the buttons: as well as necessary protection from the sun it would continue to act as a horsefly deterrent.

Far ahead I could see the Land-Rover, its solid bulk quivering like a jelly amid the heat waves and looking around, almost everything at any distance was dancing to the same silent tune. Butterflies flapped lazily past: sun loving insects, even they gave the impression of finding the temperature a little high for their liking. A turtle dove crooned briefly, like me, I imagined, too exhausted to continue. The heat was like a weight, pressing down and brooking no resistance. My blade had once more lost its edge and I stopped to sharpen it, a rasping sound ahead indicating that someone else was doing likewise. On and on we went, through the bushes and welcome grassy patches, up the slope and down, up again endlessly swinging, hacking and slashing. In one of the open areas a bee orchid peeped out from the longer grasses beside an anthill: in a few years the growing trees would shade out the beautiful flower and the teeming ants, for both need the sun. I desired only to keep as near to the others as possible, but could not resist stopping for a few moments to admire the delicate bloom before sweat rolling into my eyes blurred its beauty. Time seemed to stand still and the air vibrated with heat: the final fifty yards were a torment and no-one turned back to help me.

Jack again reached the ride first, with Ian and Snowy close behind and the rest of us straggling in one by one: I was last as usual but to my amazement not by much. I laid my slasher in the grass and flopped down against the oak, sitting uncomfortably on the cigar stone which was still in the back pocket of my jeans. Having removed it I opened my precious flask and greedily drank half a cupful of tea, which seemed to evaporate on its way to my stomach. It really was far too hot to have any appetite for food, but I managed to force down a cheese sandwich, rendered limp by the heat in its airtight box. It felt dry as powder in my mouth and almost devoid of taste. The chocolate bar I looked forward too oozed out of its foil wrapper and had to be licked up, much to the amusement of Chris and David who lay in attitudes of semi collapse close by. Conversation soon palled and I was certainly more than happy to sit quietly watching the world go by. A ringlet settled briefly on a bramble stem almost within reach: a lovely butterfly the colour of dark chocolate, with small pale circles on each wing from which its common name is derived. The reeling song of a grasshopper warbler came from an indeterminate direction and real grasshoppers chirped all about. Overhead, above the life preserving shade of the oak, the incandescent sun had burned almost all colour from the sky, rendering it virtually pale grey. Never before had I felt so hot or drained of all energy as I slowly sipped the remaining half cup of tea. It did nothing but temporarily moisten the inside of my mouth: my body needed pints of liquid.

Heat induced lethargy seemed to have overtaken everyone, even

Jack who all morning had given the impression of being impervious to it. He, like me was sitting back against a tree and still sweating, his tanned, weatherbeaten face glistening and the sight was strangely comforting: it indicated he was human after all. A horsefly buzzed round and round, a low, menacing hum before finally settling on my exposed chest. I watched it walking about, feeling this way and that with its front legs for a choice spot to bite and as its head lowered my hand reduced it to a flattened corpse. Another soon met a similar fate, but I failed to notice one which sneaked onto my elbow until it was too late, a stinging sensation advising me of its unwelcome presence. Now and then swatting sounds told me the others were also being assailed by the winged pests: indeed flailing arms provided the only evidence any of them were conscious.

The break was stretched a bit, for which I was profoundly grateful, but finally Jack got to his feet, retrieved his slasher from beneath the Land-Rover and began to sharpen it. I had noticed both he and Snowy put theirs under it, though it barely registered. The reason they did so became obvious the instant I picked mine up: the blade, which had been lying in the sun was hot enough to fry an egg and I had no choice but work a way along my row before it cooled enough to hold. A dull edge makes for hard going and instead of fairly gentle strokes I was forced to hack and swipe at even the softest bushes, further draining what little energy had been recouped during the break and the hottest part of the day was still to come: I fairly wilted as the thought entered my mind. Someone flushed a male nightjar which swooped soundlessly around us for several seconds before slipping away among the heat waves. Everyone stopped to admire him, the white spots on his dark tail brilliant in the sunlight: he must have been perched nearby, but his amazing camouflage rendered him almost invisible when motionless.

The natural world had fallen silent, beaten into submission by the heat and the only sounds were those we made: the swish of steel through grass, bush and bramble, the scratch of thorns across jeans, rasping of a blade being sharpened and muttered curses as another horsefly drew blood from unprotected skin or, perish the thought, someone inflicted 'Sheffield Blight' on another little tree. We were working across the widest part of the plantation and the rows gave the impression of being endless, the curve of the down such that the Land-Rover was well below the horizon behind us before we reached the bottom fence and the very welcome shade of tall trees. As on all previous occasions I was last to get there, but the pace had slackened sufficiently so there was time to sharpen my slasher at leisure and still lean against a fence stake to breathe in draughts of the marginally cooler yew scented air beneath the leafy bower. Two o'clock, supposedly the hottest part of the day: we started back up the slope and it felt like stepping into a blast furnace. From several parched throats came mumblings to the effect that it was too hot for work, but work on we did. Jack said it would be afternoon drink time when we reached the ride, an irresistibly appealing thought but no-one had the energy to speed up and get there more quickly. Bushes, brambles, grass: I was treading down as much as I cut, then came the dreaded 'snick' and tiny extra resistance to a stroke: the top of a beech lay accusingly beside its now bare stem in the short grass. I should have seen it, but had reached a point of barely concentrating, wishing only that I could be sitting in the shade with a long, cool, iced drink in my sore hand and wondering if such thoughts were the first stage of delirium brought on by dehydration. Unfortunately keen eyes witnessed my mistake and a chorus of derision followed, but my face was far too red with heat to register any embarrassment. Some of those who shouted loudest I had seen commit the same crime so I didn't feel too bad about it: no-one had been horsewhipped or hanged.

The sense of relief on reaching the ride was overwhelming. The experience after dinner taught me a lesson and I laid the slasher carefully in the shade, put the cigar stone with it then slumped down beside them to open my flask. The tea, black and sweet had long ago lost all its fresh brewed flavour and tasted rather of stale treacle. No matter, it was ambrosia to my desiccated palate and I drained the full cup in an instant. Only one left now and that I would save for knocking off time. No-one spoke. The smokers barely raised enough energy to make their roll-ups, but such is the power of addiction that thin puffs of aromatic smoke soon stained the air around them. How I was to survive the last stretch of the day I really didn't know, but knew I would because failure was unthinkable. For a few glorious moments I lay full length on the grass with eyes half closed, until a tickling sensation on my waist made me move. Brushing off the offending yellow ants before they could bite I rearranged myself against the young oak and sank once more into a semi stupor. Doing nothing except breathe and allow my tired body to feel it was sinking into the earth was sheer delight. Unfortunately, like all other wonderful sensations it came too quickly to an end as Jack's stentorian voice roused us to reluctant action. It seemed a very long time before everyone had become vertical and begun scrubbing at their blades, the freshness of early morning but a distant memory and my arms had never felt so stiff. "Down and up will do us," said Jack, which meant facing another hour of slow cooking beneath the solar grill.

Heat waves continued to dance crazily in every direction and the sun still boiled down from high above, but there was no doubt about it, the fierce heat had tempered ever so slightly. Conflicting emotions swept through me: I was glad, for it had been almost unbearably hot, yet also wished it would remain so until we finished because to stay the course under those conditions would mean beating a greater challenge. Flicking grass away from the first tree switched off all conscious thought processes and I was once more in automaton mode. A fresh red rash appeared across my knuckles as a gorse bush whipped back. On we went, even Jack now merely coasting along: somehow I found the strength to keep up. Dick whipped the top off a larch and not a voice was raised: I saw him step on it and look furtively around before continuing. I didn't count trees or steps or minutes, merely wished my labours could be at an end as we reached the bottom fence. A short breather and a sharp-up in the shade and we set off on our last rows, none of us wishing to delay the finish by languishing there. Another jarring of my wrists as the blade hit an old stump: this row seemed so much longer than all the others. Sweat still gushed from every pore, though I felt there could be no liquid left in me to come out. The heat was definitely easing off: it was merely very hot now and the sun had begun his slow descent to the western horizon. Somewhere close by the grasshopper warbler began again his reeling refrain. I worked on, my trees hidden amid an apparently endless array of low bushes, yet I found them one by one and all remained unscathed. Oh how slowly the Land-Rover grew larger, a dusty bronze green and limestone beacon beckoning until finally I reached the ride. It was over: I had finished! For a moment I could only stand at the end of the row, lean on my slasher and look back over the area we had covered during the broiling day, thirst momentarily forgotten.

I placed my hook in the back of the vehicle with the others, a moist, dark stain on the work polished handle providing instant identification. My burst blisters continued to weep, but had long since ceased to give any pain worth thinking about. The lukewarm liquid left in my flask required considerable imagination to believe it bore any resemblance to tea, yet the finest champagne could not have tasted better as I drank it in quiet celebration. Heat, flies, spines and prickles aplenty and a multitude of battle scars to show for my efforts: already a rosy glow had begun to surround the forming memories of this momentous day as I sank gratefully onto my uncomfortable seat and closed the door for the journey back to the yard.

CHAPTER 2
HEDGE TRIMMING

Hedge trimming didn't strike me as a job woodmen should be involved with and was certainly not the kind of work I expected in my new career: a clip round the garden with shears on a weekend was one thing, but to discover we had four miles to cut, with faghooks; that was depressing news indeed! This task I was told had its origins in the days before the First World War, when King Edward VII used to come by train to Singleton station for the August race meeting at Goodwood, or to visit the James's at West Dean house and their country hideaway near the crest of the Downs at Monkton: the routes he might use had to be spick and span for his arrival. The railway ceased to be before Dr Beeching swung his axe, indeed I remember as a boy seeing the last train puff up the line and the king was dead as the railway, yet the tradition was maintained.

When the hooks were brought out from the store a small ray of hope shone briefly: they were all cranked, right handed hooks and I, for better or worse, am left handed. Seizing the opportunity I informed Jack of this complication, whereupon he delegated me to be the sweeper, to clear up the cuttings and put them in the trailer for carting away. There were others who viewed the job with no greater enthusiasm, but they were unable to come up with a cast iron excuse for being let off the cutting detail and my escape was greeted with some mutterings, comments I encouraged by grinning at them. Alas, or so I thought at the time, my pleasure was only temporary.

We began this awful task alongside the main road, outside what had recently become the Weald and Downland Open Air Museum, though not yet open to the public where a narrow belt of trees, a 'rew' in Sussex parlance, separated the hedge from the museum ground and whose shade reduced its vigour. In places it was almost non-existent, the thorns weak and bereft of all but grimy tufts of twiggery at the top, gaps bridged with chestnut paling fence of similar height, the road and its rushing traffic but a pavement away and along this narrow strip we worked. Dirty red flags on hazel sticks were pushed into the hedge either side of us to act as a warning: there were no yellow jackets, men at work signs or cones back then. In the tree shadows those flags were barely visible at a distance: the infrequent pedestrian could see us far more easily and drivers would certainly notice the Land-Rover, tractor and trailer parked as far as possible on the pavement before becoming aware of the grubby, limp objects.

For the first day Chris had been given the job of tractor driver and sweeper, but as I was now doing the clearing up he took his place in the cutting line until such times as I filled the trailer, when he would break off to take the load away. This was the plum job, coveted by those who disliked trimming and while my left handedness gained me the most active part of the plum I never got to drive the tractor, which was a great disappointment. The gang lined out beside the hedge with about twenty five yards between each man and began cutting: for a time I had nothing to do except lean on the broom and trade good natured insults with Dick and David, who were closest to me. The system seemed to work well and progress was rapid, like a well oiled machine.

As soon as there were sufficient cuttings to make the effort worthwhile I began brushing them up, the smooth tarmac pavement making this easy. Sometimes an area had to be swept twice because the bow wave of air created by a passing lorry scattered the carefully gathered heap all over the place. As the cutters completed their sections they moved ahead of the line and started afresh. While the breaks in their labours were measured by these brief pauses, mine were more frequent and longer because a fair distance could be swept quickly and shovelled into the trailer: I then had to wait for the next lot to accumulate. I was settling nicely into this routine when a familiar figure appeared, strolling along the pavement: it was Arthur, with something ominous in his hand. After stopping for a few words with his brother Jack he came to me with what for him was an impish grin on his face. "For you," he said, handing me a brand new left handed hook: he had been to Chichester and bought it especially for me. How the grizzlers laughed and I could only share in the merriment: my cushy number was over and the joys or otherwise of trimming a hedge with a hook were now to be discovered.

I gave the broom and shovel to Chris and took his sharpening stone: a new hook is rarely very sharp and several minutes work with it were required to give the blade a keen edge, a grey dust of carborundum and steel powdering my fingers as I rubbed it. My left handedness meant working in the opposite direction to everyone else, so I walked well beyond the front man and began cutting towards him. My hands had become sufficiently work hardened there was no longer much danger of rubbing blisters, but very soon the unusual action of sweeping upward cuts made itself felt in my wrist and forearm. No matter how sharp the hook a hedge can only be effectively and neatly trimmed by cutting upwards in the direction of growth. A single stroke is easy; after a thousand the hook begins to feel heavy and the wrist, unused to the strain acquires the hedge trimmer's equivalent of writer's cramp. Bending to cut the bottom, gradually straightening up to complete the face then reaching across the top, it didn't take long to develop a reasonable rhythm. Cuttings showered down, road dust and disturbed insects filled the air. A bewildered greenfly, dislodged from a weedy piece of sycamore twisting up between two thorns, settled on my face and began walking, the irritation so intense I swatted it without a moment of thought or regret: it was the first of many. Trimming the back side was a different matter: very ragged due to lack of light and competition from the fence it required little work, merely cutting what could be reached without too much trouble.

Roadside hedges usually collect rubbish thrown or blown from the carriageway, or dropped by walkers who should know better. This one was no exception: shreds of old newspaper, browned with age and dirt were caught amid dusty leaves of ivy which crept through the bottom; an old glass bottle, capless, had become a tomb for many insects whose mouldering remains made a thick, black, lumpy soup inside. Part of a number plate was wedged between two stems, mute evidence of a past accident, and a variety of cigarette packets completed the decorations. Why is it that so many people have so little regard for the countryside that they are content to leave it resembling the outskirts of a rubbish tip?

Our breaks were endured rather than enjoyed. We sat in the Land-Rover with windows and doors closed to keep out as much traffic noise as possible until the air became so foetid and thick with cigarette smoke that we who did not partake of the weed could stand it no longer, the vehicle rocking gently on its springs in the rush of air which accompanied every passing lorry. David unwisely balanced a flask cup on his knee at lunchtime while he filled it with coffee, only for it to tip and soak his jeans when a juggernaut roared by. The resulting stream of four letter words caused a good deal of amusement, while a hand, quick as lightning, pressed the still steaming denim hard against his leg, bringing out more anglo-saxon and further laughter. There was nothing more amusing than discomfort or pain, providing it was someone else on the receiving end.

The hours seemed to fly and my initial unhappy thoughts evaporated as dew before the summer sun: I was enjoying the job and looked back with pleasure on my work, not that these sections could be distinguished from the others, even with close inspection. It all looked very neat and must have been a source of begrudged pride, even to those who really disliked having to do the job. Unfortunately the constant rush of traffic destroyed an otherwise peaceful ambience and the hiss of airbrakes was always disconcerting, particularly when we were taking our breaks as lorries slowed because something coming from the opposite direction prevented them swinging wide to pass our vehicles. I have no doubt it was Jack's choice to get this, the worst part, out of the way first: we could then look forward to several days of tranquility along the Motor Road.

Locals all knew the quiet lane by that name and it probably harks back to the earliest days of the internal combustion engine when the royal visitor was driven along it. Traffic did use it, mostly estate vehicles during the week, with the postman early morning and the daily milk tanker rumbling along some time later, but there were long periods without such intrusions. We young woodies, as we were known around the estate, took advantage of such windows of opportunity at dinnertimes to indulge in our own special form of vehicular progress to which, for reasons known only to himself, Jack usually turned a blind eye unless he was expecting a visit from Arthur. Reversing a tractor and trailer is quite simple when you know how: doing it at full speed added a certain spice, particularly if we happened to be working along a stretch with bends and Double Barn, where there is a sharp corner, was the ultimate challenge. Success required quick but delicate use of the steering wheel: a small under- or over-steer and your attempt came to an abrupt end as the trailer would jack-knife in a moment. Instant full use of the brakes in these circumstances was necessary to avoid bending the trailer drawbar. We always maintained a good lookout while this game was in progress to avoid embarrassing incidents with other vehicles or being caught out by the unexpected appearance of Arthur or the agent, who also drove alone the lane occasionally and did no damage to ourselves, the machinery or hedge. It was great fun.

Beyond The Warren the lane winds its way beneath Chequers, in the 1970s a great beech hanger, a tidal wave of deep summer green overhanging the hedge and lane, breaking on the grey tarmac shore. Wild strawberries grew on the bank: small as garden peas and packed with the most intense flavour they were eagerly sought. Pigeons crooned lazily from the green depths of the wood. Now and then, with a characteristic flurry, one would launch itself in display flight across the valley to Warren Hanger on the opposite slope, power climbing then with a clap of its wings gliding down, repeating this several times before being lost to sight amid the far beeches. The song 'Lazy, Hazy, Crazy Days of Summer' came to mind as the countryside gave the impression of being at least a little drowsy, though we sweated away at our task, flicking up the scraggy little bushes which in places barely formed a hedge, even allowing a generous interpretation of the word.

No drowsiness at Double Barn. There an old barn stood near the sharp corner: lime mortared flint walls crumbling, ancient thatch moss grown and slipping, held in place only by a filigree of rusty wire netting, most of the hazel spars as rotten as the wheat straw they once held firm. At one time there must have been a second for the place to be so named. This decaying monument to farming of an earlier age provided shelter from sun and rain for a group of young cattle, which had the run of an adjoining fenced yard and was also sparrow city. A squabbling, merry colony of the dowdy yet beautiful little birds was active all the long summer days. Some sought edible morsels amid the trampling hooves of the stock or golden grains spilled along the lane edges by passing trailers hauling corn to the drier; others dust-bathed in the yard or flattened themselves on the top rail of the fence to sunbathe; still more hopped in and out of holes in the thatch to quarrel with their neighbours. Their incessant chirping was a delight and they took less notice of us brushing up the hedge than the inquisitive cattle did, most scarcely bothering to acknowledge our presence. The old barn is now gone and with it the little sparrows; a bulldozer brought its frail remains crashing down, wormy timbers and rotten thatch lay in a heap before a match did its work. Its flinty bones returned to the earth whence they came, carted away to fill ruts in a track somewhere on the estate, a sad end for a small piece of farming history.

Leaving the tree lined sinuous valley the lane curves upward to the crest of Lodge Hill from where the rolling downland country stretches away west and north. Across the fields to the south swallows swooped and dived among the Friesian milking cows of Lodge Hill Farm. To the north lay a golden cornfield around which a combine hummed noisily and beyond, the buildings of Colworth Farm stand within a protective screen of tall trees. Ahead the lane runs almost arrow straight towards the Rabbit Warren in the next valley, hedged on both sides with quickthorn and beech. These were real hedges, not the scrappy things which edged the woods and took longer to trim. As there was no easy way to get through them some of us dealt with the back while the rest worked along the side facing the lane and we shared the top: whenever there was a choice I plumped for the back. A few years previously, on both sides of the lane new rews of beech had been planted, taking in the edges of several fields. The subsequent lack of cultivation had allowed a small wilderness of rank grasses, nettles, brambles and clematis to develop, growing up and into the hedge in spite of being cut back each year, in places covering the rusting wires of the original field fences, which had not been removed. When they were struck accidentally with a hook there came an instantly recognisable metallic grating and the blade lost its keenness, necessitating a sharp-up. Each component of the tangle produced its own variety of pain: the irritation of formic acid from nettle stings making small white bumps; stabs and tears or broken lines of blood across knuckles and forearms from thorns, prickles and corroded steel barbs, but the compensations more than made up for this temporary suffering. It was the location most favoured by birds for building their nests.

As a country boy I had enjoyed the pleasure of bird nesting each year, looking for new specimens to add to my egg collection and swapping doubles with friends for desired additions, their value determined by rarity or the difficulties encountered in acquiring them. We adhered strictly to an unwritten code that only one egg could be taken from a nest and I'm sure our hobby did little harm: it certainly taught us a great deal. My annual quest had taken me into many of the estate's woods and my feet, in smaller boots, had trodden the old lane, but now I was content merely to look at and enjoy the delicate shelled jewels we came upon in the course of our work. A hen yellowhammer flew out in alarm and I carefully parted the tangle of bramble to find her nest, a neat round construction of grass and small rootlets, its deep cup lined with grey and white hair. Three beautifully marked eggs lay in the bottom, very pale purple with spots and scribbles of dark purple brown: at this time of year they must have been a second clutch. I touched them gently with the tip of my finger to feel their warmth. Seeing me so engrossed Snowy and David came for a look and were equally appreciative of the find, which I then hid once more by drawing together the spiny stems before resuming my progress. On such a warm day they would not chill as a result of being uncovered for a few minutes: the hen would return before we worked our way much further along and the sharp eyed crow could not reach into the tangle to pillage it after we had gone home. A short distance away were the remains of a song thrush's nest from the previous year, its mud lining moss grown and crumbled, flattened by the elements and covered with the chewed brown remnants of hawthorn berries: a wood mouse had dined there many times.

Dick was working his way towards me when suddenly he stopped, saying "I'll leave that bit for you." I thought nothing of it until trimming 'that bit' when I became aware of an increasingly loud and angry buzzing around my legs: he had trodden on the entrance to a wasps' nest and sportingly left me to face their all too obvious displeasure! This was no time for bravado; an undignified and hasty retreat was called for which would have been the envy of many a sprinter. Hoots of laughter, "Buckaak, buckaak" chicken calls and a number of wasps followed me: I didn't stop to count them as I was too busy running. Much to my relief the pursuit was soon called off, the buzzing faded and I stopped to look back: either my panic had been contagious or the wasp attack more widespread than I realised, for several others were walking back to the hedge from various points along the lane. I had not been stung, an outcome which enabled Dick and me both to claim a victory, he for luring me into the trap and me for escaping unpunctured. We always kept a good lookout for these 'yellow jackets' as my father called them, yet going undisturbed about their business they were surprisingly difficult to see, rising like tiny helicopters from their front door to zoom away on foraging trips: it was the angry buzz, rapidly increasing in volume as they swarmed out to defend their nest which provided brief and nearly always insufficient warning of their presence. 'That bit' never got trimmed.

Sounds of furious activity drew our attention from inside a gateway, the scrabbling of feet and heavy thuds. A track led from the lane into the field behind the rew and trapped by his antlers in its loose boundary fence was a large, perspiring fallow buck. He stood proud and wild eyed, looking at us for a moment before attempting to leap that which held him. The stringing wires cut short his bound, bringing him down with a sickening crash into the dust his struggles had churned up. While I extricated myself from the bushes behind the hedge Snowy ran to the Land-Rover for his jacket and a pair of fencing pliers, then we set about cutting him free. He rose instantly as we approached and was again brought down by the wire and his own momentum in another flurry of dust. Avoiding wildly flailing hooves I jumped on him before he could regain his feet and covered his face with the jacket to calm him a little. This seemed to work as he lay completely still but for the rapid heaving of his beautiful spotted flanks, while Snowy crouched beside us to begin cutting the wires twisted around the palms of his antlers. At the first snip of the pliers he began to struggle and it was all I could do to hold him down until the last strand had been severed. He then stood up, throwing me off with contemptuous ease, hind legs narrowly missing us both as he cleared the now tattered remnants of the fence to run at full gallop down the hill and out of sight. Dusting ourselves off we stood to watch him go, apart from a few superficial scratches apparently unharmed by the traumatic experience: as there were no cattle in the field we left the fence for the farmer to mend. The incident was a major topic of conversation at afternoon tea break, some saying we should have killed him, others glad we hadn't; all admitting they would not have gone near him and surprised we hadn't been injured in the tussle.

Such high excitement did not occur every day, but other, smaller things were just as memorable: ripening hawthorn berries glowing maroon and rose hips a brighter red, each painted by the sun with a pinpoint reflection of light; tall grasses ripening and goosegrass seeds clinging to my shirt and jeans as I laboured through the tangle, my face red as the haws; the sun beaming down and scattered, puffy cumulus clouds, the larger ones with grey bellies sailing slowly across a wide sky the colour of a dunnock's egg before a breeze so gentle it was almost undetectable beside the hedge. My reverie was interrupted when the Massey Ferguson's muffled tickover in the lane suddenly became a purposeful hum and a puff of black smoke erupted from its exhaust pipe as David, who was sweeper up for the day set off to empty a load of cuttings. The expected silence following his departure never came because it revealed the distant hum of the combine on Colworth Farm and a continuous buzzing of insects quite distinct from that made by my personal following of sweat flies.

On this long, downhill stretch the hedge on the north side of the lane was much better than that on the south, which was rather gappy and composed partly of tall, mature hawthorns with trunks as thick as my leg and an ash tree whose roots penetrated the ground beneath the lane, causing bumps in the tarmac. Along the good side we had been asked to leave occasional strong beech shoots to grow on and ultimately become trees, a wish of Mr James. This did not find favour with us or our hooks and by accident or design, most were decapitated. To cover up the heinous crime we made sure a selection of shoots were left standing proud, but each year they were different ones so the intended trees never grew any taller. Time lapse photographs over several years would have showed these little sprigs apparently moving hither and thither, back and forth along the hedge and uncovered our game. Had they been allowed to grow unmolested into large trees the resulting dense shade would have killed the hedge beneath, an outcome none of us wished to see happen which probably explains the serious outbreak of 'Sheffield Blight' in that area. Nothing was ever said, but I still wonder if the agent or Mr James noticed the trick.

When we reached the foot of the slope I knew the job was nearing its end, and the 'hooking' season also. It was with some sadness I looked along the final stretch to the junction with Hylters Lane because I had thoroughly enjoyed the trimming; however, I also looked forward to starting some real forestry. One last hazard remained to be negotiated: there were bees at the bottom of the hill. An apiarist from Chichester kept several hives in the rew on the south side of the lane. They weren't close to the hedge, but one of their flightlines passed over it rather too close for comfort. Keeping an eye on the small dark shapes zipping past a few feet above my head I trimmed as fast as possible, hoping all the while they didn't take umbrage at my presence: the ire of fifty thousand bees was something I had no wish to experience. Chris, on the opposite side behaved rather like a partridge having seen a hawk, ducking and whipping beneath the danger zone as fast as he could while still trimming. The two way traffic was continuous and having sharper eyes in those days it was easy to see the homeward bound foragers looked larger than those setting out because their pollen sacks were filled. Happily they remained more concerned with transporting their golden burdens than stopping to attack us and we were soon in the clear.

Chapter 3
Finding my feet

I watched enviously as trees were felled and trimmed out, the hum of chainsaws echoing through the woods, but I was only allowed to carry the fuel cans, sledge hammer and wedges: it was very frustrating. Perfectly sensible of course, because I had no idea how to use one and little comprehension of the potential dangers associated with their use. I could only look on as the others worked, try to learn from their actions and mistakes, stack cut wood and hope. Look on I did, drinking in every movement, every twist and turn of their arms as they reduced a tree to bare trunk and a scatter of cut limbs, which I had to stack. Looking back, the time spent as general dogsbody was very important and I learned a tremendous amount about the job, including the most simple things. The hammer and wedges were always placed on the stump after a tree had been felled so they could be seen by everyone and didn't get lost among the ground vegetation. The fuel cans were kept a safe distance from the action so they could not be flattened by falling trees, but I didn't need telling why they had to be well away from fires. Trees were felled, not chopped down: to do that you used an axe. A chainsaw has a bar and chain, not a blade. No-one shouted "Timber!" when a tree fell; they always made doubly sure we all knew what was happening and were well out of harm's way before the point of no return had been reached. Shouting like that was something they only did in lumberjack films: in real life it didn't give anyone close by time to get out of the way.

Forestry, in common with most occupations, has its own language. Lots, parcels and cube; hoppus feet, breaks, sinks, claws and moors, cuckoos and benders, widow makers: they soon became familiar terms and understanding their meaning brought me one small step closer to becoming a woodman, at least I thought so. Knowing the words is one thing; acquiring the skills an entirely different matter. My opportunity to use a chainsaw finally came at Seven Points where we had to cut a quantity of beech timber, a parcel of 3000 cube Jack told me. A cube was another term for the hoppus foot, the closest to a cubic foot it was possible to get using a girth tape to measure round timber. I had been given no indication this was to be a momentous day: it began as others had with me fetching and carrying as required while more exciting activities went on all around. I was working with Snowy, stacking the four foot lengths of cordwood he cut when he switched off his saw and handed it to me saying, "See how you get on." I had longed for this moment since that first day in July and was overjoyed, but tried to maintain an impression of it being just another job. I doubt he believed me. All chainsaws are right handed, but only at this point did it occur to me that there might be a problem Arthur could not overcome so easily with a quick trip to Chichester.

I held it with some trepidation and was pleased to find it didn't feel awkward, only strange. A Stihl 045, pale grey and red with an overall covering of dust, the bar bereft of paint through much use: the weight seemed very light compared to the larger pieces of cordwood. He showed me how to hold it properly, twist it this way and that, which parts of the chain to cut with and a variety of helpful hints, then stood back to give me space. Most of the woodies drop started their saws, a technique frowned on these days by the health and safety police, but no-one ever had an accident as a result. I tried and failed, not being able to judge how hard to pull the cord while effectively throwing the saw away from me with the other hand and a second attempt fared no better. "Use a bit more muscle," said Snowy and I did: it burst into life, ticking over sweetly after emitting a puff of blue smoke. I revved it up several times, the momentum of a rapidly moving piston causing it to buck slightly as the motor accelerated. Snowy had trimmed out a couple of limbs so I only had to cut them into cordwood. Nothing could be simpler, after all I had watched the same thing being done many times. Pressing the throttle cautiously the chain began to move and I touched it against the grey green bark. It stopped. "More throttle," said Snowy, so I revved it right up before making another attempt. The chain became a shining blur as the cutters bit into the wood and a spray of chippings shot back against my right leg and boot: the limb sagged slightly then fell away from the trunk, or butt as they were known in the trade. Success was very short lived: I made a second cut and the chain jammed, the engine labouring to continue driving it and smoke began coming from under the clutch cover. "Let go of the throttle, it's pinched," said Snowy quickly as I mentally curled up in embarrassment. I did and the engine resumed a happy tickover. The smoke ceased but the bar remained immovably stuck. I pressed the stop switch. The cut had closed because I failed to notice how the limb was held up either side. He picked up a piece of cordwood to use as a lever and lifted it, opening the cut once more and allowing me to pull the saw free. That was my first important lesson: nothing was quite as simple as it looked and I would need to recognise when wood was under tension or compression. In subsequent years this knowledge saved me from possible injury on many occasions. He then showed me how to make a cut with the top of the chain from underneath the limb so the wood effectively fell away from it. This time the saw started first pull of the cord; I made a successful cut and managed the rest of the limbs with no further trouble. A glow of satisfaction tingled through me and I'm sure my smile went from ear to ear. We stacked up before joining the others for afternoon drinktime.

I was dogsbody again when we began thinning and converting in the Windens, put with Ian to stack for him. This brought with it many more new terms and some very hard labour. I didn't realise it at the time but there was an unspoken initiation process somewhat on the lines of continuous assessment: it lasted months until a newcomer either made the grade or fell by the wayside. Here I was tested by having to keep up with a fit, skilled 'woodie' intent on earning good money by piecework. The plantation had been thinned several times before and divided into strips called cants, with narrow, tractor width 'racks' between them where at first thinning lines of trees had been removed. Each sawyer worked along one cant and the cut wood had to be stacked at each edge of it, beside the racks so it could be picked up and hauled away. Beech, Scots pine and larch, Douglas fir and Sitka spruce; cordwood, stake lengths, six foot one butts for larch lap fencing, seven foots for strainers, slim eight footers for struts, four foot mining timber, Bowaters - four foot lengths of beech up to ten inches in diameter destined for Bowater's pulp mill in Kent - and wood wool: each product to be stacked in separate heaps. Ian hammered away with scarcely a backward glance and I was determined not to be left behind. The heavier pieces I had to upend several times to get to the racks because I couldn't lift them and sweat poured from me. Sticky conifer sap covered my hands, jeans and shirt; a mélange of fragrances to which adhered a good deal of dust and dirt. There was barely a moment to stop and watch what he was doing and by hometime my arms felt as if they had lengthened by a foot. This went on for several days and I was finally forced to pay the doctor a visit, getting signed off for a week with back strain. Ian's grin when I returned said a great deal, but he admitted he could not have kept up the killing pace much longer and we made a good team from then on.

When several cants had been completed Ian and Chris began hauling out the produce, each with a tractor and trailer: everything was loaded by hand in those days, so this was no easy option. I was sent to stack behind Snowy again and after a few days he continued my chainsaw education by letting me fell my first tree, a small beech. I cut out the sink as he directed to aim it then made the back cut. Slowly it began to lean, gathering speed as the angle increased, brushing its way between adjoining trees to land with a loud swishing sound on the damp ground, the draught sending leaves swirling away and disturbing a yellow underwing moth. Yippee! Cutting it up was completed slowly and without incident then beginners' luck ran out once more. Next was a larch and it cuckooed, became snagged on a good beech. I looked at Snowy with the question "What do I do now?"

written across my face. He smiled and asked me to cut the butt end clean through at the stump if I could without getting the saw pinched, so we could strike it back. Using an eight foot pole as a lever we worked the butt off the stump and backwards. It gouged a furrow in the ground, each shove increasing the pile of earth building up against it and soon we could get it no further: the tree remained firmly stuck. "I'll have to cut it back," he said, taking the saw. Using a measuring stick he marked the tree for a six foot one butt, sawed partly down from above and finished by cutting up underneath to ensure the wood didn't split and the saw didn't get trapped. The two cuts met perfectly, the timber parted cleanly and the end of the trunk hit the earth with a soft thud, shaking the beech but not letting go. Repeating the process achieved the desired result and slowly the crown slid free, falling with a long drawn out crackle of breaking twiggery. "You can trim it out," he said, handing me his axe. Larch branches are brittle and small ones can almost be brushed off the butt with a good stick, though an axe makes a much neater job. This practice was a relic of the days when axes and a variety of big hand saws were the woodman's toolkit and their use gradually faded away, but I am glad I had the opportunity to experience a little of the old ways. My boots may have had steel toecaps, indeed they were our only protective clothing at that time, but I took great care not to swing the blade towards my feet as I worked along the butt, stopping where it became too small to make any of the products we were cutting. Snowy cross cut it and we did the stacking together. Next day I felled a few more trees entirely on my own: real but slow progress.

Chris was away the following day and as there was insufficient Bowaters hauled out to the loading area in Sandy's Bottom to fill the lorry expected that afternoon I was asked to take over his tractor, a four wheel drive Fordson Super Major. While disappointed not to be cutting I was very pleased to have the chance to drive this lovely, battered piece of machinery, my previous experiences all being on two wheel drives with the Nature Conservancy. Its blue paint was faded, scratched and scarred with rusty streaks, its mudguards dented, there was very little tread on the tyres and its power steering was slack.

A horseshoe had been wired to the radiator grill with two pigeon feathers stuck in the mesh to complete its decoration. Chris had left it at the loading area and I was dropped off there with the ignition key while the others went on in the Land-Rover. He had put a plastic sack over the seat to keep it dry overnight - there were no cabs or even roll bars in those days. I tucked that away, checked the diesel, oil and water levels then sat down to begin the day. The engine barked into life, the rather stubby exhaust covered with strikes from air rifle pellets making it sound as if there was more than fifty five horsepower under the bonnet. The morning was still and trees threw the sound back at me as I trundled along the bottom track. Loading had to be done going downhill because the tractors could not pull a full trailer up the steep, and in many places slippery, racks. Quite how slippery the slope was I soon discovered when having selected what I judged to be the correct gear and opened the throttle wide the tractor came to a scrabbling halt half way up, the almost bald tyres not finding sufficient grip in the mud. Stamping on the brakes to change into reverse it began rolling back: they couldn't hold it and I was unable to get it out of forward gear. The descent was made with the brakes on and clutch pedal depressed, raising it to spin the wheels each time I felt it was going too fast. Somehow I reached the bottom, still facing uphill with the trailer jack-knifed, having had a bit of a scare. A second attempt, aiming this time for ground which had not been driven over was successful and I had no trouble getting to the top, wondering at what speed I would be descending later with a heavy load behind!

The trailers were large enough to put on two stacks of Bowaters, one behind the other and to get on as much as possible we used pins, eight thinner pieces of pulp, to increase the height of the stacks. They had a safe working load of thirty hundredweight I was told, but it was normal practice to put on as near to three tons as could be managed: this cut down the number of trips, saving a lot of time and they appeared not to suffer any harm from this abuse. I drove carefully along the rack which Chris had been hauling from, stopping at the first pulp heap I came to. Only beech was used for Bowaters: a few pieces of oak could sometimes be sneaked into a lorry load, but too much would mean

Hauling Bowaters with the four wheel drive

having the load rejected because it adversely affected the quality of the pulp. Four feet long and from three to ten inches diameter, the weight of individual pieces varied widely and I soon realised it was sensible to load selectively, putting the larger pieces on first to avoid having to lift them higher than absolutely necessary. There had been rain during the night and the humid atmosphere within the stacks proved very attractive to slugs: I knocked many off with a flick of my finger rather than squash them, much to the amusement of Dick and David who were working in the cants either side of me. The trailer sides sloped outward and with the wooden pins in place there was little room to spare going along the rack. Loading was actually a good deal harder than stacking on the ground because even the largest pieces had to be lifted and as the load grew so did the effort required. It took almost an hour to put on all I thought the trailer could stand, sustaining grazed knuckles in the process when a heavy piece slipped and jammed my hand against another. I finished off by chaining the front stack on to prevent it slipping forward and spilling over the tractor if anything went wrong: all that now remained was the descent.

Driving to the top of the slope I stopped and made the necessary preparations, setting the throttle at tickover to provide maximum engine braking. Selecting first gear I eased off the handbrake, put my heel on the diff lock pedal and set off. No problem, at first. The engine speed increased a little as I expected then the tyres lost their precarious grip and away I went, sliding all the way to the bottom. Happily, Chris had been down several times and created a good set of ruts which the wheels followed: there was little danger of hitting a tree, but it was still a heart fluttering few seconds of bumping and banging over exposed roots. From behind came a cheer as I slithered to a halt, thankful the load hadn't moved: David witnessed the show and pointed out that it had not been in four wheel drive. I must have kicked the lever back at some point when getting on or off and not noticed. Another lesson learned.

Recovering my composure I stopped beside the Land-Rover to collect my lunchbag and put its strap over the mushroom shaped air pre-cleaner protruding through the bonnet: I'm sure its designer could never have imagined it being put to such a good additional use. The steady run down to the loading area provided a few minutes of relaxation, mentally and physically, tractor and trailer rolling gently from side to side on the potholed flinty track. A roebuck stood in the deep green shadows, watching me go by, confident I presented no threat. It was very likely he didn't realise there was a human on the noisy object or he would have been away, barking as he ran. The sun made pools of golden light along the ride, splashing me briefly with warmth as I drove through them. Speckled woods fluttered from the brambles as overhanging runners were touched by the muddy wheels and a few flowers lingered on a patch of tall foxgloves. Summer was drawing to a close. Chortling loudly a cock pheasant launched himself from the ruts as I turned out of the plantation. His end might come before Christmas, but this day he could display his bronzed beauty without fear of attracting a deadly charge of shot. I stopped between the two depleted stacks of pulp, from which several lorry loads had already been taken and pulled the engine cutoff. For a moment after the rhythmic clattering ceased I could hear nothing, but small sounds soon became apparent. A wren sang from nearby bushes and there was a faint hum of unseen insects. To have my morning break before unloading seemed a good idea. Placing my flask cup on the diesel tank filler cap behind the steering wheel, I lodged my sandwich box in the spokes of the wheel, slid forward in the seat so I could lean back and put my feet on the tank: life was great.

Three tons had been put on the trailer, now three had to come off. It took less time to unload because I wasn't continually getting on and off the tractor to drive from heap to heap. My intention to save at least some heavy lifting in the plantation by putting the heaviest pieces on the bottom was a good one, but it didn't save me having to lift them a second time. However, standing on the trailer bed I was over two feet from the ground so able, when I picked these lumps up, to throw them higher on the rising stack without too much effort. This also meant less straining later when the lorry arrived as they were closer to the height of its trailer bed. I was almost finished when Ian arrived on the David Brown with a load, the sound of its engine almost overwhelming the clonk of wood on wood as I transferred the last few pieces to the stack. We agreed another load each would be more than enough to fill the lorry, though there were a great many more tons to be brought out. I left him unchaining and returned to the plantation to get my next one.

The lorry came mid-afternoon, just as I finished unloading my third trailer full. I passed the time of day with Dave the driver then left him reversing between the stacks to give Jack the news, passing Ian coming out as I drove back to the gang. The hum of two stroke motors died as this not altogether welcome news spread and everyone made their way to the Land-Rover carrying their saws. Though we were a long way from any public path they were never left in the woods: the light fingered fraternity can turn up anywhere, at any time. I took the precaution of putting my lunchbag in the vehicle because it was unlikely Jack would think it worthwhile returning to the plantation for a few minutes work after we finished loading. For me and Ian there was the imminent prospect of lifting some of the pieces for a third time. The artic could take over twenty tons: with eight of us plus the driver loading that would be around two and a quarter tons each. We had already lifted nine tons twice so would go home having picked up the equivalent of a full lorry load each.

The empty lorry looked enormous as we stood between it and the stacks, four on each side. Ian reversed his trailer against the rear end so his load could be transferred direct and we set to work. The 'thonk' of wood against wood rang across the loading area, providing an almost rhythmic accompaniment to the merry banter which never failed to develop when the gang were together and able to talk. The stacks began shrinking once more as they were transferred piece by piece to the lorry. At first progress seemed incredibly slow, but it wasn't long before the shorter members of the gang were having trouble reaching the top of the rising load, particularly at the front of the trailer, which was higher than the rear. One by one they left off, climbing onto it to take pieces handed up and stack them neatly in place. As the load got higher so it became ever more important to ensure it would remain in place for the journey to Bowater's pulp mill in Kent. Those of us still on the ground also found it increasingly hard to reach the top with the larger pieces and began 'two-ing' them, one end being thrown up and the other pushed on upstretched arms until taken by those on the load. I closed my eyes each time I was pusher to ensure they didn't get filled with falling debris. To finish off the load was tied in by putting a line of pieces down the centre, resting equally on each stack: they would prevent any slippage when securely roped and that was the driver's responsibility. It took us about an hour to put on what Dave estimated was twenty two tons: he had no wish to be obviously overloaded in case he was stopped by the police. At the mill he would get a weighbridge ticket for the estate which would prove how accurate his estimate had been and added to the quantity of timber already sent away that week, allow Arthur to calculate how much piecework money we had earned.

While those on the load clambered down, we in the ground party brushed ourselves off and admired our handiwork. It did look a neat job and Dave was pleased: pieces hanging out in all directions can make a load unsafe and attract the eyes of the law. He roped it down while we broke out our flasks for a welcome drink, before joining us for some idle chatter and jokes. It was a great pleasure to relax after the strenuous exertion, feeling mildly strained yet not tired: how different from that first day in July. We continued to sit and enjoy a few more minutes of the late afternoon sun as he departed on his journey to Sittingbourne, saluting us with a blast of his air horn as he disappeared down the track.

We were back in the Windens again at the end of the year, thinning a compartment closer to Sandy's Bottom. By this time I had been given a saw and was considered competent in its use, but on Christmas Eve 1970 I realised it was a mistake not to have sharpened it before we went home the previous day. Snow had fallen early in the morning and the ground was whitened: when the Land-Rover stopped no-one made any attempt to get out, waiting for Jack to make the first move. As he opened the door a wave of arctic air came in, producing a mass involuntary shiver and a variety of expletives about the temperature. The heavy grey cloud bore a slight purple hue and a thin east wind cut like a knife. Those with sharp saws went speedily to work, the deep hum of 050s soon dueting with the lighter note of 045s, the combination sounding much like a very large swarm of bees in the wood. Silently cursing myself, with already cold hands I picked up my toolkit and took out the round file: the chain had touched a stone during the last cut I made yesterday: it had only done slight damage but meant the cutters would not bite in as they should. Buttoning my donkey jacket up to the neck and putting on my gloves made not a great deal of difference; the wind still preferred to go through rather than round and my hands soon became a painful mass of pink and purple blotches. It was true boss's weather; a day when everyone would work as hard as possible simply to keep warm.

I did the job as quickly as I could but was shivering like a leaf before I finished. It was a great relief to file the last cutter, put the toolkit away and for a few moments wave my arms about while jumping up and down in an attempt to restart the circulation to my extremities: both fingers and toes had gone beyond painful and were virtually numb. I almost ran to where I left off the previous day and started the saw. The encounter with the stone happened while crosscutting a larch and I had been unable to complete the tree: now it lay beneath a thin blanket of snow. Each cut produced a shower of pulverized crystals amid the chippings, which dampened my legs and somehow found their way up my right sleeve. Cutting finished I took off my gloves so they would not get wet handling the snow covered wood, waved my arms about a bit more then stacked the cut lengths. The blotches on my hands started to fade and be replaced by redness as warm blood began to course through them again, a process curiously assisted by the icy snow which wetted them. A couple more trees and they had come through the pain stage, glowing with warmth inside their thin leather and fabric cocoons, but only so long as I kept working: my toes remained merely cold.

The sun came out for a time but it began snowing again later in the morning, almost imperceptibly at first. Tiny slivers of ice slanted down through the trees, glittering silver and gold as they passed across the sun's pale disc, hissing gently onto the carpet of frozen, snowy leaves. Jack called lunchtime and one by one the saws stopped. I stood for a short while listening to the tiny sound of the snow, the crunching of seven pairs of boots making for the Land-Rover and beyond, the silence of Christmas Eve in the whitened woods. I am not religious in a church going sense, but there was something special in the bitter air, something indescribable with which no amount of present buying, pre-Christmas bingeing or praying and singing in a cold, stone building could compare. I was in my cathedral, the sound of falling snow my hymn: for those few moments at one with everything around me and wanting for nothing.

CHAPTER 4
THE PICKLE YARD

Rain lashed against the windscreen as I drove to West Dean. The weather folk had promised us a wet day and this usually meant confinement in the pickle yard, the place and jobs least liked by almost everyone, so it came as no surprise to hear this was to be our destination as we gathered in the yard, each arrival hurrying to join the increasing huddle sheltering in the Land-Rover's shed.

The estate produced all its own wooden fencing materials and treated them with creosote by heating in a long tank filled with the pungent black liquid. From this process did the small ivy encrusted, tree girdled old chalk pit beside Grinch Lane get its name. There was no rush to alight as the vehicle stopped in the sloping, rain soaked, creosote stained pit: even the air held a noticeable tang and by hometime so would our clothes and hair. A choice of three jobs awaited us: splitting and pointing, peeling or dealing with the pickle tank and its needs, the latter normally done by Joe or Jim with such help from us as required. Standing down in the stokehole revving up the fire beneath the tank, its base protected from the flames by sand and steel plates, was certainly the warmest and driest place to be, but it was a job requiring care and a thermometer. The creosote had only to be heated to about 80 degrees Celsius; if it reached boiling point it would bubble over the sides of the tank and down into the fire, instantly creating an inferno from which the stokers would be lucky to escape without at least a singeing.

The round poles cut for stakes, strainers and struts were usually debarked mechanically in the woods, but the machine couldn't remove every vestige. After the stakes were made by splitting and pointing in the pickle yard the clinging remnants were stripped by hand using drawknives and billhooks under a roof of corrugated sheeting which covered the line of 'breaks – waist high frames to rest the stakes on while they were stripped – and the pickle tank itself. Everything was impregnated with creosote: the woodwork was black, in some places dull as though sooty and in others shiny as if varnished; wall mounted lights glowed a murky yellow and if the wind was unfavourable, acrid fumes from the tank and smoke from the stokehole chimney made it an eye watering place to be. Such was my lot this day with Ian, David, Jack and Dick, while Chris and Snowy were making the stakes with a McConnel circular saw beneath a similar roof on the other side of the pit: they at least only had an occasional waft of diesel exhaust from the engine and ear jangling scream of the blade ripping through wood to contend with.

The job and Hades-like atmosphere combined to ensure productivity was low. No-one had the slightest enthusiasm for the work, but there was fierce competition to pick up the straightest, cleanest stakes as they could be finished easily with a few swift strokes of a drawknife; knobbly, uneven ones took longer. Time seemed to pass incredibly slowly, but the pile of white, cleaned stakes grew as they were stacked in tens, each row at right angles to the preceding one so air could get between them: only by being seasoned for a while would sufficient water evaporate from them to allow creosote to be absorbed when they were 'boiled' and allowed to cool in the tank.

Jack, after completing a couple dozen, drove off for a meeting with Arthur, the general consensus being they would spend a few minutes discussing work before getting down to the more serious business of drinking tea. No matter, the work rate slowed in inverse proportion to the increase in banter, while from across the pit came frequent screams from the throbbing McConnel, aural evidence that Chris and Snowy at least had not slackened their output. Joe soon had a good fire going in the stokehole and before lunchtime, our mid-morning break, creosote fumes were beginning to rise like dirty steam from beneath the sheets of tin covering the eighteen foot long tank to keep out driving rain and prevent anyone falling in, adding to our misery.

Jack really must have forgone tea drinking after his meeting for he returned within half an hour and became, for me at least, the good fairy. "Have you got your waterproofs?" he asked. "Yes," I replied quickly as a glimmer of hope flashed through me, instantly lifting my spirits. "Good, you can get a load of stakes from the Windens; jump in and I'll take you to the sawmill." The tractors and trailers were always parked under cover there. I was to take the four wheel drive and big timber trailer to bring back as many five foot six inch stake lengths as could be safely put on and chained down.

The tractor had lights but the trailer didn't, not that this was of much concern to us in the 1970s unless we had to be on the road after dark, when a Heath Robinson arrangement was cobbled together and tied on its rear end to warn anyone coming up behind of its presence. It was daylight, if rather gloomy, and I saw no need to switch them on as I set out clad in waterproofs and sou'wester, overjoyed at escaping the infernal atmosphere in the pickle yard, no matter how bad the weather and gleefully aware there would be much grumbling from the boys still confined. Though I steered round the most obvious puddles, almost as much water came upward, thrown by the tyres as was falling from the leaden overcast, and in minutes it was running down my coat, making a puddle on the seat in which I had no choice but to sit: at least my overtrousers were waterproof. Leather and fabric gloves were not and soon became soaked: they kept the wind off but did nothing to repel the raw cold.

The main road and first part of the Motor Road were fairly well sheltered by woods and it was actually quite pleasant cruising along at the tractor's maximum speed of about fourteen miles an hour, engine humming and clattering smoothly in that familiar Fordson way, raindrops exploding into steam on the hot exhaust pipe. On reaching the crest of Lodge Hill however it became a good deal less so for the rain came almost horizontally on the wind and I pulled the brim of my sou'wester down as far as it would go in a vain attempt to prevent drips finding their way inside the upturned collar of my coat. A welcome respite through the coppice woods of Brickdean till past The Beeches then in the open again at Stapleash Farm it was even worse: the milking herd had been walked along the lane, leaving mud and a liberal scattering of sloppy dung which I didn't notice until too late. The tyres threw up the resulting slurry, spraying me from head to toe: it is amazing how much solid matter can be trapped by a beard, moustache and eyelashes!

To reach Sandys Bottom and the shelter of trees again was a very welcome relief; the rain fell vertically once more and I was no longer being hosed from one side. Drops fell heavily from the tall Douglas firs beside the bumpy track as I cruised slowly along to the junction where I turned left into Winden Bottom: I could see them but the engine noise rendered the gentle plops as they hit the saturated ground inaudible. Rivers of water, grey brown with suspended chalky mud, hurried down the wheel ruts, splashing out to either side as the tyres temporarily interrupted their flow, the tractor rolling and swaying gently on the uneven track as I drove deeper into the plantation, climbing gradually all the while.

The heaps of peeled poles were at the northern end of the wood, not far from the estate boundary nearly a mile from Sandys Bottom. Rain continued to fall heavily, creating a thick greyness between the trees, though deep in the valley there was little wind. Beeches, larch, spruce and fir; all seemed to be standing motionless, wooden shoulders hunched in resignation as water dripped from every twig, leaf and needle, running in tiny rivulets down boles darkened by moisture and the dull grey light. Their massed ranks threw back the sound of the engine, a continuous echo keeping pace with the tractor, ceasing the instant I pulled the stop button, having turned round and reversed to the required heap. My ears having been assailed for more than half an hour by wind, rain and mechanical noise suddenly found themselves in what seemed to be total silence but quickly became attuned to the lesser sounds of a wet day in the woods. High above on the valley sides wind rushed through the trees sounding very like the constant crashing of surf on a beach, swaying their tops back and forth with its buffeting while around me there was only the steady drip and patter of raindrops on my wet, cold stiffened Barbour waxproofs. My gloves were running water and useful now only to keep my hands relatively clean. I took them off, finding as expected that my fingers were white tipped and crinkled due to the cold and wetness.

It was dinnertime and the gang would be sitting in the foulness of the peeling shed bathed in creosote fumes, or the Land-Rover where cigarette smoke would quickly render the atmosphere equally foul: I would enjoy my drink and bite sitting on the tractor in the rain, there being nowhere dry to go, the diesel filler cap serving its usual function of table for my flask cup, opening my lunchbox briefly to extract a sandwich then a piece of cake. While by no means hot I was not cold either, but didn't spend very long refreshing the inner man. Rain splashing into the cup of steaming tea cooled it noticeably while I ate and took the occasional sip, though it remained pleasantly warm and flavoursome to the last diluted drop. Replete, I squeezed out the sodden gloves, put them on and stepped down to begin loading, sinking to my ankles in deep, rutted mud.

Having brought the big trailer I could put on a considerable quantity of five foot sixers, sufficient to make several hundred stakes when split and pointed. As the largest would only make four decent stakes when sawn down their length none were too heavy to lift comfortably, any pieces of greater diameter had been cut into seven foot lengths to make strainers which I didn't have to take and loading was rapid at first. Each clonk of wood against wood produced a dull thud rather than a ringing echo which they would have done on a fine day, their wetness and the rainy atmosphere together effectively deadening the sound. I could feel a sweat building up inside my more or less waterproof cocoon, though shirt collar and cuffs were already uncomfortably wet from rain which inevitably managed to find a way in. Feeling clammy in such conditions is not pleasant, though it was good to be really warm, particularly my toes which in wellingtons had appreciated the journey out even less than my fingers did.

As the trailer was wider than the poles were long I stacked them down the centre to maintain stability and leave a narrow strip of clear bed either side: standing somewhat precariously on this enabled me to build the load with ease much higher than I could from the ground, though the double handling involved did slow things up a bit towards the end. The limit was decided for me by the height of the pins at the ends of the trailer and length of chain I had to tie the load down with: when the top formed an even curve like the crust of a well risen loaf I considered it enough and stopped for a quick breather before unwinding the chain, looped neatly over the numberplate mounting behind the seat. One end had a substantial hook which I put under the front of the trailer chassis before throwing it over the poles and walking round the back to dog it down, the top logs creaking slightly as it tightened on them, holding the load nicely firm.

Rain continued to fall heavily as I climbed back on the tractor, kicking the footrests to dislodge some of the mud from my boots and sweeping most of the accumulated puddle from the seat with one saturated, grimy glove before sitting down. For a few moments I listened to the rushing of the wind high in the treetops and steady patter of the rain then started up for the journey back to the pickle yard, the wet exhaust quickly steaming dry as it barked hot defiance at the weather. I was buoyed by the thought of the welcoming warm fire in the stokehole which I could stand by to dry off once the unloading had been done before returning the tractor to the sawmill. I would seek no help with unloading: it would have been churlish to ask the others to get wet when there was no need and only add to their misery. Already the sweat was cooling and would be an unpleasant damp feeling long before I got there. Before driving out onto the road once more I stopped to check the load in case lurching and bouncing down the long bumpy track had loosened it: it was fine, but I managed to tighten the dogs by one link so it had settled slightly. Press studding my jacket up to my neck again and pulling my sou'wester down to cover as far as possible the right side of my face for the return trip I set off, remembering to drive more steadily past Stapleash Farm to avoid a second coating of slurry.

My stay in the pickle yard had been short on this occasion, but

I wasn't always so lucky: many are the times I have gone home at the end of what seemed interminably long days absolutely stinking of creosote. It is one part of the estate for which I have no fond memories, though amusing things did occur very occasionally. One day we had to pull over a small sycamore which was cut because it was in danger of fouling the yard's electricity supply wires. Though several of us pulled on the rope it fell sideways, brushing heavily against the wires and causing them to gyrate wildly for some moments, inevitably contacting each other. At each touch there came a shower of crackling sparks, visible as far along the wires as we could see down the hill towards to the village, but the power stayed on and therefore we felt no need to call Southern Electricity. I imagine their engineers would have been less than pleased with our unintentional attempt to weld the wires together and replaced them, but am certain the damage remained undiscovered for years. There was one event which could have had far more serious consequences, for the yard if not those involved, and it is the only act of deliberate stupidity I can recall taking place in all my time on the estate. One of the other gangs had been sent there for the day and seeking devilish amusement had deliberately over stoked the fire under the pickle tank, with the inevitable result that it boiled over, creosote pouring down the sides of the tank onto the fire and causing an inferno to which the fire brigade had to be called, luckily arriving before too much damage was done. Most of us wished in our dreams we could destroy the place but not in our wildest moments would we have made any attempt to do so and found it difficult to have much sympathy for the perpetrator, whose name will remain so far as I am concerned unknown.

CHAPTER 5
THE SAWMILL

The prospect of spending a day in the sawmill, possibly an entire week if Jim or Joe was on holiday, was viewed with only marginally less gloom than that which descended as a result of being incarcerated in the pickle yard by bad weather. There were no poisonous creosote fumes and plenty of fresh air because three sides of the long, low building were open, but it was not a hot place to work except in high summer and due to poor lighting the corrugated steel roof held beneath it a dullness, even on sunny days while the yard in wet weather was a shallow soup of mud and bark fragments. It did have one redeeming feature much liked by everyone; a small hut at the far end, also roofed with corrugated sheets, in which were seats, coat hooks and an open fireplace. A single cobweb draped window provided the only illumination inside when the door was shut unless on cold days when a fire blazed in the well used grate and projected our shadows as flickering silhouettes onto the board walls; then such a fug of heat built up it became all too easy to doze off. Beside the fireplace two toasting forks made from twisted fence wire were leant against the well worn, dusty brickwork: they were made much use of to produce toasted sandwiches and to dry wet gloves.

The heart of the mill was a great bandsaw which utilised four inch wide blades running vertically on three foot diameter wheels and below them was a deep sawdust pit, board covered so the sawyers couldn't fall in. A long, power driven rolling bench which could be moved back and forth through the saw supported the logs to be cut and behind it was an open framework onto which sawn boards could be pushed for temporary storage. The saw was electrically driven and had to be brought up to operating speed through three stages by juggling the switches: it was all too easy to misjudge the timing required and it would cut out, necessitating a restart, sometimes more than once. There was also a large circular saw, like the bandsaw run by electricity, though in earlier years it had been belt driven from a stationary tractor: this we knew as the raise and fall, probably because when the blade was turning one edge went up and the other down. Timber brought in for cutting on the bandsaw was unloaded on the dock, a series of raised baulks which were at almost the same height as the saw bench so they could easily be rolled onto it with canthooks over bearers laid across the intervening space.

One fine, sunny day it was my misfortune to find myself there again helping Joe as Jim was away. A load of Douglas fir and larch logs filled the dock, having been brought in on Bill's lorry a couple of days previously: they were to be turned into 4"x2" rails and other fencing requirements, plus several large beams for repairing a barn. Though we didn't like the place it together with the pickle yard were vital parts of the estate's infrastructure, supplying almost all its processed timber requirements.

Before starting the saw Joe wanted the accumulated sawdust cleared out of the pit as it was nearly full. After removing the cover boards I picked up a shovel and the first of a number of plastic sacks then stepped into it and began digging. It was soft and had settled in layers of different colours rather like sedimentary rock as a result of cutting several species of wood. A strong mélange of pleasant fragrances rose from it as I shovelled and soon the square space was clear but for small quantities in the corners I couldn't get out with so large an implement. Joe was satisfied and together we replaced the boards then carried the sacks round the back of the hut where a fire burned almost constantly to dispose of such waste, tipping out all but one which was put aside because someone had asked for a sackful to

The sawmill in 1978

use as bedding in their pet rabbit's hutch.

Joe had put a fresh blade on before he went home the previous day so it was sharp and needed only to be tensioned: it was always slackened off overnight or when not being used to reduce strain on it and the wheels. One more small but important thing had to be done before we could begin sawing: the blade required lubrication. It ran between thick felt pads enclosed in small cast steel pots with lids which acted as reservoirs, the lower end of the pads adjusted to brush lightly against it: they needed to be filled with diesel which slowly seeped through the felt, lubricating and helping to keep the blade free from sticky resin which would otherwise cling to it and greatly reduce its effectiveness. Nowadays this is illegal and water is used for the purpose in all modern bandsaws. I didn't take up Joe's offer to let me start the saw: he was familiar with its eccentricities but still had to go through the sequence twice before it reached cutting speed and settled into its characteristic loud metallic whirring. I ran the bench back until it lined up with the dock then we put the two strong, tapered bearers across and with a quick twist of a canthook the first log rolled obligingly over: they weren't all so cooperative. While Joe held it against the moveable fence I slid two curved steel dogs into their holes on the front of the bench and swung their pointed ends smartly over so they bit into the log and fixed it in position. He then moved the fence well back so it would not be in the way when the first, waste slab was cut.

I was very glad of my earmuffs from the moment the saw worked itself up to speed: at that time I was the only one who possessed them because they were essential when pistol shooting, which was one of my hobbies, and safety helmets hadn't yet made their appearance at West Dean. They effectively eliminated the damaging effects of the high pitched scream the blade made as it cut and it baffled me that Joe was happy to work without any. The log, a very nice twelve foot length of Douglas fir, had been well trimmed out in the woods but one or two small sharp skegs had escaped the chainsaw and the heel of my hand discovered one as I leaned against it briefly before Joe flicked the lever to start the bench moving, tearing up a tiny flap of skin which for a few moments hurt out of all proportion to its size. The bark was covered with resin filled blisters and I amused myself by popping several as the bench moved slowly along, the pale coloured, viscous liquid sticking to my fingers and I painted a blob onto the tiny wound to staunch the barely perceptible seepage of blood before inhaling deeply of the wonderful fragrance it gave off. The blade finished its cut and the first slab dropped away from the far side of the log. Joe stopped the bench and we slid it onto the wooden rack behind the saw before he reversed the bench to its starting position ready for the next cut. I swung back the dogs while he held the now unstable log then gave it a small push so that it fell with a weighty bang onto its newly cut flat surface.

Standing by the ends of the log we pulled it towards ourselves until it was positioned so that the bottom of the next cut would just meet the edge of the first to produce a square corner and I swung the dogs over again to hold it. Once more the long, loud scream and the second slab dropped away. We repeated the process a third time and had then reached the point where we could begin cutting out sized timber. Joe swung the fence towards the blade slot which ran the full length of the bench and set it at two inches then we pushed the log hard against it. He had part of a finger missing, the result of a mishap years before when he forgot to move his hand from the line of the blade and it was cut off in an instant. I was surprised he didn't lose some more because it was his habit to hold the log against the fence until the very last moment, keeping his hands a mere hair's breadth from the shimmering teeth it appeared from where I stood as the bench moved forward and I hardly dared look. We lifted the first board onto the rack: it still had one uncut, waney edge as did the bulk of the log. With that stage complete they were stacked back on the bench with their straight, two inch edges against the fence which had now been set to cut eight inches wide and ran them through the saw. This removed the remaining, waney edges which we took off and threw out onto a pile in the yard before running the bench back, setting the fence to four inches and making a final cut. Ten pristine lengths of 4"x2" now lay in a neat pile on the bench. Douglas timber is a lovely pale pink, the outer wood sometimes equally pale yellow, and it seemed almost sacrilege at that moment to sully the clean surfaces by touching them with grubby hands. They, like the waste pieces, were bound for the pickle yard, the first to become fuel for heating the tank and the 4"x2" to be put in it.

Timber felling, weeding; indeed most of our work could and sometimes did become tedious after a while. In the mill, as in the pickle yard, I was mentally prepared to be bored stiff from the start: this frame of mind and the thought of spending the day there while the sun shone, knowing everyone else was out in it, did not help the time to pass quickly. Unlike hedge trimming, where during the first day of swinging a faghook I discovered great pleasure was to be had, no such feelings developed here and the days seemed to grind on very slowly. I liked Joe and got on well with him, but the hours spent there felt as though they contained many more minutes than those which governed our work in the woods. Looking back on these long gone days, and there were quite a few over my early years in the department, I picked up an ability and indeed a love of working with timber in this way which lay dormant until thirty five years later when, as a reserve warden for Hampshire and Isle of Wight Wildlife Trust, I persuaded my employers to purchase a Wood-Mizer mobile bandsaw so I could process timber from my thousand acre patch for our own use and to make products as a source of income. There is something intangible but very satisfying about turning a rough and uninspiring piece of timber into useable posts, boards, rustic benches and even fine furniture. Wood has been man's friend and provider of shelter, tools and construction material for hundreds of thousands of years: it is a wonderfully tactile material and it gives me immense pleasure still to be working with it in a small way.

There were occasions when our visits to the mill were less onerous: going there to get one of the tractors; bringing in a load of timber; making use of the hut and its welcoming fire to dry off after some wet job among them. Now and then over the years it became the scene of horseplay. It had been snowing and Keith's gang were confined in the pickle yard while I had been out firewood cutting with mine and we decided to make a raid on the others before drying off at the mill: foremen could still enjoy a little carefree fun now and then. Filling the back of the Land-Rover with snowballs we drove into the yard where I turned round ready to make a quick exit and we leapt out, throwing a barrage of slightly slushy balls at our defenceless targets. As they rallied and began to reply in like manner we swiftly departed for the mill and barricaded ourselves in the hut. A bad move: not many minutes passed before we heard Keith's Land-Rover draw up and the sound of boots approaching. A grinning face appeared at the window then more footsteps were heard round the back and the sound of scrabbling as someone climbed onto the slippery roof. In a matter of moments smoke began to come back down the chimney and spread across the room because they had blocked it with a slab of wood. We endured it as long as we could but it rapidly became so thick we could barely see the window and crouching down close to the floor made no difference. Choking and with streaming eyes we knew there was no choice but to open the door and make a dash for our vehicle, expecting to be snowballed as soon as we emerged and all the way to it, as indeed we were.

Small dramas also occurred. I forget now why we were there and cannot find the relevant day in my old diaries, but our sudden appearance in the yard startled a small flock of house sparrows which had been sitting on the mill roof: they were always about picking up woodlice, earwigs and beetle larvae which fell from the timber or taking advantage of grain spilt in the farm yard over the fence where Home Farm's friesian dairy herd stood twice each day while waiting to be milked. All the birds flew off except one, which in spite of furious flapping was unable to get airborne. Fetching a ladder I got up onto the roof to see if I could help him and discovered one of his toes was caught in a small tear at the edge of a corrugated sheet, his struggles having torn its thin skin down to the bone. He protested loudly and pecked harmlessly at my hand as I gently restrained him before trying without success to free the toe. I always kept a penknife in my lunch bag and after several fruitless attempts to ease the toe out called for someone to fetch it and I freed him by cutting it off: there was no alternative as we had no means of trimming back the steel other than a sledge hammer and wedges, the use of which would have frightened him to death and possibly seriously injured him in the process. After waiting a few moments to see how he reacted to the amputation I opened my hand and without a moments' pause he flew swiftly away, only slightly the worse for wear I hoped.

CHAPTER 6
THE GREAT BEECH

The harsh, powerful bark of the Stihl 090 Lightning ceased, allowing us to hear once more the gentle tickover of the Perkins engine in the winch tractor, rear wheels lifted clear of the ground on its anchors, thick silver thread of steel rope taut between it and the huge beech. A puff of dirty blue smoke rose from its exhaust as Chris opened the throttle and started pulling. Slowly the great tree began to tilt: as wide as it was tall, a faint swishing of air through the enormous canopy increased in volume as it gathered speed, continuing to fall under its own weight, the winch rope slackening as it was outpaced. For a few seconds time seemed to stand still as we watched in silence, safely beyond the danger zone, then came a long, earth shaking, splintering crash as limb after limb broke under the force of impact, piling one onto another, the sounds echoing back from across the park meeting those still made by the collapsing tree. A rush of air filled with dust, debris and smoke from the nearby fire rolled away in a tidal wave, momentarily enveloping Chris as he sat hunched, head down with his back to it on the tractor before dissipating into the open parkland beyond. With a fading crackle of breaking twiggery and the ends of branches still intact flailing wildly, the tree settled: it was as if half its mass had disappeared, swallowed by the earth. Close to where this magnificent specimen and its neighbours once stood students at West Dean College now park their cars. I cannot remember if they were diseased or simply swept away to create space for the future, but hope it was the former. We had already felled and trimmed out one of the veterans, but this was the largest of the group and setting about its fall no five minute job: it took almost half an hour from the moment Ian started the big saw.

The first step was to get a rope up it, actually a steel sling or wire, they all meant the same thing. Its great cauliflower shape made tipping it with a sledgehammer and wedges virtually impossible and the only way to get it down would be to winch it over. David, our most confident climber, was unanimously elected to do this and went to get the sling while two of us raised the ladder, extended it as far as possible and slid it up between the massive lower limbs to rest on the broad trunk, ensuring the top sat evenly on both rails at its maximum extent. With one end over his shoulder, a shackle through its eye he climbed, the sling dangling down behind him and paused at the top. It would have to be attached higher up to ensure the winch could pull it, while he needed to decide on a safe route to climb which would also allow him to pull the sling up when he had shackled it round the tree and throw the free end out through the branches. Only by doing so could he ensure it wouldn't get caught under any when it was connected to the winch rope and strained up: a straight pull was essential and would put least strain on the winch. He climbed several feet more then holding on to a small branch with one hand slipped the sling off his shoulder and swung the end round the trunk, the heavy shackle dropping conveniently over a limb within reach: often it took more than one attempt to do this on a large tree so we were fairly impressed, though shouted up only derogatory comments about beginner's luck. With the sling attached he pulled the free end up, loosely coiled it and made a throw: this time his luck failed and it caught on a branch, slumping down close to the trunk. Ripe comments followed as he pulled it up to try again, successfully this time, and the loose end hung swinging a few feet from the ground.

While he returned to earth the sling was connected with a 'C' hook to the winch rope eye: this was a forged piece of former axle over an inch in diameter shaped like the letter from which its name

The winch tractor and the great beech

was derived and weighed almost as much as a sledge hammer head. As soon as he was down we removed the ladder and Chris began preparing for the pull, driving off to a safe distance, the rope reeling out as he did so. He stopped after making sure he was square to the line of pull – it is easy to roll a tractor if pulling hard at an angle other than through its long axis – and began taking up the slack. When the rope started to tension the tractor rolled back a short distance until its four wide anchor spades dug in to the ground and its rear wheels lifted a foot into the air. Chris flicked on the ratchet brake and stopped pulling as the rope strained tight as a guitar string. The tree shook slightly and all was ready.

The Lightning blared into life and Ian began removing the claws, as we called them. Most trees could be felled with this great saw and its three foot bar by simply cutting out the sink then making the felling cut, removing the claws afterwards, but this one was so large they had to be removed first. Slowly he worked his ear battering way round the butt, stopping several times for a fill-up because the 120cc engine was thirsty when working hard. Snowy helped to pull them away once cut free, tumbling them among the gnarled roots because they were too heavy to move any further. When the last was heaved clear he had created a level platform wide enough to walk on all the way round. Chippings from the saw lay thickly like cream snow amid the roots and discarded claws: there must have been sackfuls of them. The trunk above was now more or less cylindrical and his next job was to aim the tree directly at the tractor by cutting the sink at 90 degrees to the winch rope. This great lump, like a segment from an enormous orange, required Ian, Snowy and the assistance of a crowbar to lever off the platform and down onto the roots. Finally he was ready to begin the back or felling cut, having filled up again to make sure he didn't run out of fuel part way through this, the most critical part of the job. Snowy assisted him to get the saw absolutely level by making up and down motions with his hand before stepping away to watch as the chippings flew and the long bar with its shimmering blur of cutters bit into the stout trunk for the last time.

There was undeniable pleasure watching this giant being felled, seeing the sawyer's skills in action as Ian once again worked his way round the trunk and wishing it could have been me wielding the saw, but there was also sadness. For two centuries the tree had withstood everything nature could throw at it; winter gales and hot summer sun, frosts and rains. It had witnessed the endless comings and goings of man and beast, sheltering many generations of stock beneath its broad canopy, but it possessed no defence against sharp steel. Now it lay amid its own wreckage, a thick, almost solid carpet of broken limbs and twigs, a wooden whale to be sawn and lifted, stacked and burned into oblivion. As soon as the dust settled and smoke from the fire was once more rising vertically in the still air we picked up our saws and set into the enormous task, one which was to take six of us two days to complete. Three more fires were lit, one at each side, the third at its head to burn the twiggery, broken fragments and small branchwood. All the limbs were cut into four foot lengths and stacked two feet high as cordwood, these heaps eventually measuring almost two hundred and fifty feet in total, sixteen cord, over thirty tons of firewood surrounding the great trunk which was neatly trimmed to a huge, lumpy grey green, tapering cylinder and more than enough to keep many households warm through the winter. I could barely see over the lower end of the butt, which was lodged slightly clear of the ground on its now purposeless gnarled roots. Graham and Tony, the timber haulers, would come and carry it away to West's sawmill, but even their powerful Matador crane, an adapted wartime four wheel drive lorry, would be unable to lift it in one piece.

CHAPTER 7
SQUIRREL POKING

While rabbits, hares and voles barked and destroyed newly planted trees, grey squirrels began attacking them when they had grown to pole size, stripping the bark from beech and sycamore in spring and early summer and effectively ruining them as future timber: if the stripping girdled the tree it would die above that point and the economic damage could therefore be highly significant. In some years bark stripping was particularly severe and in an attempt to reduce their numbers we went drey poking in winter during my first years in the department. While this was carried out in our own time, initially we could use the Land-Rover and the estate provided the poles, cartridges and gave us 10 pence for each tail produced, having to hand these to Arthur each week so we couldn't claim for them twice. After a year or two the cartridges and bounty were withdrawn and it became little more than a woodies' perk as it had been realised the activity reduced numbers only for a few weeks and had no effect whatever during the critical damage period. We were unable to begin poking until the pheasant shooting season had ended and attempted to cover all the woods and larger outlying copses before unfurling leaves made it impossible to see dreys or dislodged squirrels.

It had been wild and wet all night and there were no signs of any improvement in the rough weather when Ian, David and I met in the yard at eight o'clock on Saturday to spend the day poking in Church

Clump, Chequers, part of Old Reid, and an area of oak between there and the Rabbit Warren. Rain lashed the wood and the trees, their trunks wet with rivulets of water trickling down swayed drunkenly, though it was merely an ordinary gale. This was the kind of day which, had it come during the working week would have seen us confined to the pickle yard or the slightly less awful sawmill as conditions were not suitable for outside work, particularly tree felling. Squirrel poking at the weekend was a different matter and the inclement conditions, though a nuisance, might provide us with an opportunity to make a large bag as it tended to keep them in their dreys, though this could in no way be guaranteed.

We had a set of eleven hollow aluminium poles, each five feet six long and very light, one with a steel fork in its top end for poking out the dreys. However, slotted together and pushed up a tree to reach high ones they felt a good deal heavier: then the arms began to ache and it wasn't only the trees which swayed. Trying to control the column of poles, sixty feet high when we used them all, was an acquired art and had something in common with reversing a very long single axle trailer as the top would go in the opposite direction to that in which the poker moved his end: in the gale it was even harder to aim them accurately because dreys became moving targets. We began full of optimism, Ian offering to do the first poke of a promising drey in the fork of a tall, rather bushy beech while David and I stationed ourselves on opposite sides of the tree, shotguns loaded and ready, pointing safely at the wet grey sky. When disturbed from a drey, a squirrel will normally either run off through the canopy or attempt to hide by flattening itself against a branch on the opposite side to the perceived threat: having two guns so placed took away this option, though the squirrels which did so didn't usually live long enough to discover their error. Ian managed to thread the poles up though the tangle of branches and gave a couple of gentle taps on the side of the drey which protruded from the fork, at which point we half raised our guns and had thumbs on the safety catches ready to flick them off in an instant. Nothing emerged so he tapped a bit harder, finally giving a great heave which tipped the drey out and in spite of the wind it fell almost vertically to land with a solid thump on the rain sodden leaves. An investigation with the toe of my boot proved what the heavy sound had suggested: it was wet right through and hadn't been used for a long time. The most likely dreys to contain squirrels were nice firm, rounded twiggy ones, well lined and insulated against cold and wet, indicating they were winter built while the leafy ones, mostly at this time of year flattened by rain and the beginnings of decay, had been constructed back in summer and were rarely used except as boltholes when cover was urgently required. This one, the part of it we had been able to see from the ground, looked promising and fairly recent, but it wasn't: a few twigs sticking out of a mass of dark, rotting beech and sycamore leaves proved it to have been made months before.

We walked on taking turns to be poker, dreys good and bad producing nothing, the constant blanks becoming a bit disheartening. It was normal practice to completely destroy every one we poked so they could not be used again and make it easier in the following weeks to see where new ones were being built: this policy also ensured any young they contained could be killed, not left to starve. My turn came round again and I unloaded my gun, put the cartridges in my pocket and propped it safely against the leeward side of a nearby tree to lessen the likelihood of water running into the barrels before picking up the first poles. This drey wasn't particularly high and the fork touched it when I had eight lofted. My first light tap on the bottom produced a slight shaking of the twiggy ball and a squirrel emerged at high speed, making off without a second's hesitation towards the topmost twigs. David fired, the shot momentarily blotting out the sound of wind and rain: small chips of bark flew from the branch around it and the squirrel fell lifeless, landing a few feet from him. It was a buck, with a large set of accoutrements to prove it. As there was no longer any bounty paid on tails he placed his body among the roots of the tree: destructive pests they may be but he was still deserving of some respect. A foraging fox would soon find the easy meal. Scouring the majority of Church Clump produced only two more occupied dreys and two more squirrels: it was very slow going and we stopped for some much needed refreshment: if they weren't in their dreys where did they go during bad weather?

The shelter afforded by the Land-Rover was very welcome: we weren't cold but constant wind and rain are a little wearing after a while, particularly if there is virtually no squirrel activity to break the monotony of unrewarding poking. Raindrops drummed on the roof and peering through the windscreen was much like looking through frosted glass, with a layer of condensed water vapour from mugs of steaming tea, wet waterproofs and breath quickly forming on the inside for good measure. Our gloves, in my case mittens, were soaking wet and heavily stained from contact with the poles: I gave them a good wringing out before putting them on the wheel arch. The tips of my fingers, having been unprotected by the woolly layer, were also grey black with ingrained aluminium, as were our guns. There was unanimous agreement that it would be a waste of time to look any further here and having fortified ourselves we drove on to give Chequers a go, together with the young plantation of beech and larch at Double Barn. There we were amazed to draw a complete blank: all the dreys appeared to be old, leafy ones, some reduced by the elements to little more than a few twigs and the threadbare skeletons of leaves whose substance had been eaten away by fungi and small creatures like woodlice. It was a bit depressing: a genuine lack of squirrels would mean there was likely to be less bark stripping in May, but we were fairly sure this was not the case and believed they were simply playing hard to get.

The Land-Rover bucked and swayed gently through the potholes as we drove along the Cinder Track, rain sweeping in grey veils across the fields along its open side, massed trees waving before the wind in the Rabbit Warren on our nearside, all external sounds temporarily blotted out by the rattle of loose poles on the bare metal floor and hum of the engine. They returned the moment we stopped and with slight reluctance got out to resume our quest in Old Reid in an area of oak, many of the trees clad to varying degrees with ivy, and several large cherries which for some reason were free of its evergreen grasp. I made the first poke, putting two squirrels out from a compact, small football sized drey supported as much by ivy as the tree it was growing on. One went upwards and was speedily dispatched by Ian, the other vanished into the ivy close by the drey and I had to prod the area to make it run. A fusillade of shots followed: a squirrel running along crooked limbs constantly changes direction and can be very easy to miss, though each year, as a poking season progressed, our shooting speed and accuracy improved. Four were required to bring its flight to an abrupt end and its body was placed with the first among the trees' roots. A buck and doe: they would produce no more youngsters. David poked the next and three squirrels emerged, running off in different directions. I shot one and reloaded, Ian got the second and David had time to load his gun before we jointly accounted for the third, having already loosed off three cartridges to no avail. Things were definitely looking up.

A pink flash of sheet lightning lit the heavy overcast, the rain increased and a loud crack of thunder rolled across the heavens. We went on, suddenly very conscious of the guns and shared load of poles carried under our arms, potentially mobile lightning conductors though far from being the tallest objects in the wood. Another flash, quickly followed by an ear splitting crash and the rain became hail rattling down with furious intensity, the stones three eighths of an inch across dinging loudly on the poles and gun barrels. They were of two types; knobbly spherical ones composed of many smaller pieces and others shaped like agrimony seeds or minute parachutes, their rounded ends clear ice and the points opaque. The wind gusted and swirled with stormy menace, suggesting it would be sensible to leave the poles and make a hasty retreat to the Land-Rover where the battering of hailstones on the roof made conversation difficult but the clammy, cold metal cocoon felt suddenly very welcoming. Thunder continued to boom and roll for several minutes, but there was only one more flash of lightning and the hail soon reverted to rain, the wind slackened a little and, praise be, tears began to appear in the cloud through which showed slivers of pale blue: the storm had swiftly reached a brief, noisy climax and was moving on. It felt noticeably colder when we opened the doors than it had minutes before and the rain was finally petering out. A rapid drop in temperature is common in such volatile conditions and the hail still lay thickly like a dusting of snow as we resumed our rudely interrupted quest. Sunbeams began to spear through the increasingly ragged stormclouds, lighting up the rusty brown leaf litter, here and there turning water droplets hanging from the drooping tips of ivy leaves into jewels of incredible brilliance, the rapid improvement lifting our spirits. The thunder gradually muttered away into the still murky distance, dragging its wet, grey shirt tails with it. We finished the day with sixteen squirrels and were more than happy to pack up at four o'clock, though our rain stiffened waterproofs had more or less dried off and the afternoon was largely sunny. It was by no means a record bag.

CHAPTER 8

TO COLLEGE

For years it had been the practice at West Dean to send youngsters off for a six week course at Newton Rigg, the agricultural and forestry college near Penrith in Cumberland as it then was. This was something I wasn't looking forward to: three years in the Woods Department had taught me a huge amount and I didn't really feel I would learn anything very useful in a part of the country where the Sitka spruce was king, not realising until afterwards the choice of establishment was intentional to give us an opportunity to see and learn about an entirely different type of forestry. I kept my head down, but one morning in 1973 as we gathered in the yard Arthur announced he had booked me in for the Woodman's Certificate course which was due to start on September 24th. On that evening I registered at the college, having driven up over three days in my Land-Rover by a rather meandering route, stopping frequently to visit interesting places, enjoying the changing scenery, sleeping and cooking in the back and receiving an early morning visit from the police on the third day to check the vehicle hadn't been dumped! At that moment I was parked in a lay-by on the outskirts of Kirkby Thore, a few miles from Penrith. This had once been part of the main road, which now ran in a cutting thirty feet below and from my elevated position I was able to enjoy breakfast while watching a number of lapwings feeding in the fields on the other side. Suddenly they were joined by a flock of more than forty golden plover! This was very exciting: I had never seen more than a handful on any occasion previously around Chichester Harbour during winter when they migrated south to escape the cold northern weather and I helped with the Birds of Estuaries Enquiry wader counts. Shortly after they were joined by a heron, then five mallard flew across the field and a sparrowhawk zipped along the lay-by, perching nearby in an ash tree: maybe the six weeks would not be so boring after all.

Only when all the students had arrived and we gathered in what was to be our main classroom for introductions did it become obvious quite how good and wide ranging on the job training at West Dean really was: some had never driven a tractor; others could barely use a chainsaw; one or two had no experience of anything other than a mower and had never even hammered in a stake! The course would provide them with training not available in their jobs, while for me it would only broaden my range of experience, I thought. However, any feelings of superiority I harboured were immediately quashed the following morning when we were introduced to nursery work, about which I knew nothing: West Dean had once possessed a nursery but by 1970 all planting was done with trees bought in as required. Potting conifer seed and planting out seedlings in long straight lines were not the most enjoyable tasks I've ever been involved with and the weather was cold. The nursery was like an enormous vegetable bed, filled with long lines of trees ranging in size from newly planted seedlings to those more than a foot in height and ready for sale. For the planting out exercise we worked in small groups, digging a six inch wide trench, its depth determined by the length of root the tiny trees had and making sure one side was vertical, then holding the seedlings equally spaced against this side and replacing the soil, treading it down firmly. This was followed by tree identification and chainsaw maintenance and again the limits of my knowledge soon became apparent: I could tell spruce from fir but not why it was one or the other – "Picea (spruce) have pegs" is a phrase I still remember and refers to the little stubs remaining on a spruce twig when its needles are pulled or fall off. The principle of two stroke engines was interesting to recap but had little bearing on daily maintenance and that I was thoroughly familiar with. In the evening I wrote in my diary "There is a great deal more to being a woodman than any outsider (or anyone who hasn't been here) can possibly realise." It was the first of many lessons these six weeks taught me.

At that time upland forestry was still entirely focused on planting spruce and I found the policy difficult to accept for a number of reasons, not least that creating the massive, almost sterile blankets did such damage to the ground. To my mind the deep ploughing and obsession with drainage were offensive and showed no respect for the earth, a view I hold to this day. That they were considered necessary indicated many unsuitable areas were being planted; steep, rocky slopes and boggy ground where the likelihood of producing a future crop of good timber was extremely remote and its extraction almost impossible. An example lies fallen, tangled and rotting not many miles from where I sit writing in Northumberland, the trees lying across stone walls which once marked the boundaries of fields and it is one of a great many throughout the uplands. The aim to produce more of our own timber was a laudable one, but to simply throw grant money and tax breaks at what with a little more thought could be seen as destructive, wasteful and ultimately doomed projects was sheer folly. One of our field visits was to a plantation, in the centre of which was a small floating bog: how sad to see stunted, deer browsed little bushes of Sitka and Norway spruce attempting to grow in the waterlogged ground which shook like a jelly when we jumped up and down on it. The trees would fail, but drainage would also ultimately destroy the bog. No matter, every acre planted was one more towards the unattainable target of self sufficiency in timber and nothing must get in the way: in too many places implementation of the project has proved a complete waste of trees, time, manpower and ultimately money, while providing hardly a cubic foot of timber in recompense for the damage caused to the earth and displaced or destroyed wildlife.

The course covered a wide range of subjects; some familiar like brashing, which is the removal of low limbs in a young plantation before it is thinned for the first time to create access. Though they have no prickles, the hard, spiky Sitka limbs covered with those little 'pegs' made it feel much like trying to bash a way through thickets of thorn and all sorts of irritating dust and debris found its way down inside my shirt collar. We were required to do this with pruning saws, not billhooks which I had used before: they made a neat job and left no protruding sharp skegs to lacerate our knuckles on. Small larch limbs can easily be knocked off with a sharp blow from a billhook or even a stout stick, but these did not give up so easily: chopping them off would have made for extremely slow progress and produced ragged stubs, no good if you were on piecework. It was a much warmer occupation than anything we did in the open, windswept nursery: scarcely a breath of wind could penetrate the dark ranks of pole sized trees and the welcome physical activity generated a good deal of body heat. The feeling of being comfortably warm was often lacking because whatever we did outside involved a lot of standing around while things were explained or demonstrated and many activities took only half a day, frequently less, even the most strenuous providing scant opportunity to build up a good head of steam.

Machinery was naturally a popular subject and the college had all manner of tractors and agricultural machines, some specifically designed or modified for forestry use. We spent time studying various operators' manuals and doing normal maintenance tasks, checking fluid levels, changing engine oil and greasing where required. This again was something I had done quite a lot of, and repairs to ours at West Dean, though this was one subject not covered: here such work was carried out by college technicians or agricultural engineers, not inexperienced students. There are so many possible causes of breakdown or damage an entire course would be needed to cover the subject in any meaningful way and no establishment is going to damage its expensive equipment deliberately. Everyone looked forward to the session where we would have an opportunity to drive some of the more interesting pieces of kit – a more or less standard farm tractor, a small Holder forestry tractor which articulated in the centre and could turn in little more than its own diminutive length and something much larger which was called a Skidder. This appeared to be an extensively modified Ford tractor with four big wheels and was covered with armour plating, had a dozer blade on the front and winches mounted high on its rear end. This imposing piece of machinery acted like a magnet and we all wished to have a go on it. I finally got the chance and enjoyed a few minutes trundling round the yard and driving over a few bumps, which gave me no idea of what it was actually capable of doing, but its size was impressive and I felt certain it could handle most things. Little did I know how familiar to me one of its kind would become in the not too distant future.

Felling with bowsaws struck me as a pointless exercise, but in such a way was one afternoon spent, trimming out the fallen poles with axes: to someone used to doing the entire job with a chainsaw it seemed we were returning to the past for no good reason, but like all coins it had two sides. I would never be called on to work in such a way at West Dean as it was far too slow and in any case could only be used to fell small trees, but others might and in later years the ability did prove useful to me. Working with Conservation groups which all use bowsaws and other hand tools, I needed to be able to show complete novices how they could safely fell small trees, helping them get more from their activities and reducing the likelihood of injuries or practical difficulties. At first glance putting a shoulder against the tree and pushing towards the saw as I made the felling cut seemed to be a certain recipe for getting the blade pinched, but it remained free running and my weight helped to direct the fall. Another lesson learned. We also did some chainsaw felling, working in groups of three. On one occasion my group was given a little Stihl 031 to use and it proved to be nothing but trouble: initially it started with no difficulty but would not run properly, then the starter cord broke and finally the starter dogs played up which meant nothing happened when the replacement cord was pulled. It didn't say anything positive about the quality of maintenance carried out by college staff but at least the chain was sharp. By two o'clock we had managed to fell only two trees! I found the entire day extremely frustrating and annoying.

Forest mensuration was a new subject to me: at West Dean so far as I was aware we felled as many trees as were needed to produce the desired volume of timber, measuring the felled butts at the end of each day until the total was reached. What volume of timber a stand of trees could be expected to increase by in a year, calculating standing volume of groups and single trees seemed irrelevant to me at that time and indeed were in my kind of forestry because our hardwoods did not grow as regular, tapering poles. These subjects were the purpose of several field trips and we spent hours with tapes setting out sample circles, measuring and recording, occasionally getting different results having repeated the same exercise, which rather baffled us. Back in class these columns of figures were used to look up the answers from relevant books of tables: it was a mighty relief we didn't have to find them by making complicated calculations as I for one would have taken forever to do so. We measured standing heights using a piece of equipment called a hypsometer and compared the results with our estimations obtained by standing a stick of known height against the tree then walking away until we thought we were where the top would hit if the tree was felled: that meant we were looking up at approximately 45 degrees at its top. How many stick lengths were needed to reach the butt, multiplied by the length of the stick then gave the approximate height. This had to be known before the volume of timber in a tree could be calculated and possessed the distinct advantage of being equally accurate – or not – in metric and imperial measurements, depending only on how you cut the stick, but volumes could only be determined with any degree of accuracy on straight, regularly tapering conifers. With the variably shaped, frequently branched trees I was used to height and volume bore little relationship to each other, which was why we could not work out the volume until the tree had been felled and trimmed out and we were able to measure the clean butt.

Good days and bad days, wet and windy ones; occasionally some sunshine: the course proved overall to be very enlightening even though a great deal of time was actually spent doing nothing of consequence. The exam felt as though it was a far off, unreal event, but suddenly it became imminent and we spent the last two days revising, reading and re-reading our notes, studying books from the college library and for light relief playing billiards in the common room. It was noticeable that one or two of the group spent more time potting balls than poring over biro covered sheets of A4 and someone ripped the baize with a misdirected cue tip: maybe this was due to nerves. The great and dreaded day finally dawned: the exam itself was to take place at Holker Hall near Ulverston at the south end of the Lake District which meant we had to be up early to make the trip. Because the college coach was unavailable we travelled in two minibuses and the one I was assigned to gave a good deal of trouble on the way, frequently spluttering and stopping: we eventually arrived with barely five minutes to spare. I managed to keep my nerves under reasonable control throughout the day, did everything the examiners asked, to my satisfaction at least, and was able to give what I fervently hoped were correct answers to all their questions. As we were tested individually there was no opportunity to observe how others were coping, not that I was very concerned for their fates during those tense hours, and it was an enormous relief when my grilling had finished. I had done the best I could and now had only to wait to learn if I had been successful. Before we would be told we had to get back to college and the trucculent minibus decided to make my group's return as drawn out as possible by continuing its spluttering, halting progress. We dismantled and reassembled the carburettor in a lay-by and pored over the distributor to no avail: after many halts it finally stopped for good and we had to push it into Kendal, probably the warmest, most concentrated physical exercise of the course! A phone call to the college eventually brought another minibus to our aid and we left the dead one to be sorted out next day, finally getting back at 10.30pm. It had been a very long, tiring day but all this was forgotten back in the lecture room when the results were announced – I had passed!

I had become a qualified woodman, with a certificate from the Royal Forestry Society to prove it and no qualification obtained before or since means more to me. Woodmanship can trace its origins far back into prehistory, before metal had been discovered, and I consider myself privileged to be a part of that immensely long tradition. We may have modern machinery and put wood to many more uses than our distant ancestors could possibly have imagined but this substance, so versatile, so tactile to handle and beautiful to look at when worked and polished, has not changed since those remote times: I believe the men wielding stone axes, medieval carpenters too, would have held the same feelings for it as I do and got the same pleasure from working with it, even though they were unable to earn a piece of paper to prove their skill.

CHAPTER 9
THE HURRICANE

"Seven killed as 100mph gales sweep Britain" was a headline in the Daily Mail on January 17th 1974, reporting events of the previous day. We had been confined to the pickle yard that morning because it was wet and windy, but the rain temporarily ceased by dinnertime providing all the impetus needed to leave the creosote Hades and resume timber felling in Warren Hanger where we had been working the previous week. That at least was the plan as we drove up the chalky, grass centred track to the plantation, past the bramble and bush clothed old chalk pit we knew as the Rubbish Hole in which lay hidden all manner of country refuse, piles of flint and a few other remnants, the bones of what had once been Scouts Cottage. Water was still running down the ruts, spraying out as the Land-Rover's tyres interrupted its passage, but hope that we would be able to get on evaporated the moment we stopped: the trees were waving around like cornstalks before a summer breeze, several lifting at the roots. At that glum moment Jim arrived to tell us a fallen limb was blocking Binderton Lane. Not exactly welcome news, clearing it would at least delay our return to the pickle yard, where we had been unaware quite how strong the wind had become.

It buffeted the Land-Rover violently as we drove down the main road and played games with the windscreen wipers, occasional raindrops exploding as they hit the glass with the force of liquid bullets, engine working hard to keep the vehicle's brick-like shape speeding into the blast. The limb was in fact the complete top of a beech which had been snapped off where rot had created a weakness and completely blocked the lane. We cleared it with one eye on the rew in case anything more fell unheard above the roar of wind and hum of two chainsaws, its stump like a jagged, broken tooth still standing among the other madly whipping trees: it was now very obvious this was far more than an ordinary gale.

So wild had it become Jack decided to drive up to Seven Points, checking the road en route to see if anything else needed immediate attention. With the wind now more or less blowing from behind we bowled along in fine style and a much lighter boot was required on the throttle to maintain momentum; the petrol consumption must have been considerably reduced and the buffeting was far less fierce. The main road and Singleton Hill were clear apart from a few pieces of twiggery, but four trees were down at Seven Points and a fifth fell as we arrived. Three of these belonged to Goodwood Estate; our two had crashed through the wooden paling boundary fence, reducing sections of it to matchwood and were blocking the narrow lane to Seven Points house. As the occupants, if they were there, which was not very often, did have an alternative, treeless way out we decided it would be foolish in the extreme to attempt working on them as things were and turned back, more trees falling behind us, being almost flung down by the force of the wind. Four had been blown over at St Roches and another handful fell before we came away, none of which touched the road so could all be left for another day: it was in any case too dangerous to stay, though strangely exhilarating watching untamed nature unleash her full, unstoppable fury on the woods. The roaring of the wind was tremendous.

The pickle yard began to seem almost friendly as it beckoned us to spend the last hour of our working day in its gloomy confines, but again the wind intervened. A tree had been blown down across the lane to Colworth Farm and this would require the winch tractor's muscle as well as saws: Jack took me to the sawmill to get it. Rain was falling in earnest as I drove up Grinch Lane, past the pickle yard, my eyes continually switching their nervous gaze from the lane to the waving trees on either side, to find the gang already well on with trimming out the fallen one, sprays of saw chippings flying along with the horizontal rain and clinging all over their wet waterproofs. We moved only what lay in the lane then cut the butt from its upturned roots so I could pull it clear, the detached moor falling back into the bowl shaped depression it created when the tree toppled and therefore no longer a potential danger to anyone who might stop to look at it. With the job done as far as was immediately necessary – it could be finished off another day when the storm had passed – we returned to the yard, more than ready to go home. Frank came round the corner and asked me to leave the tractor there, not take it down the mill in case it was needed again.

It was, almost immediately: a tree had fallen into the road at St Roches. Knocking off would have to be delayed. Though the rain had temporarily ceased it was an unpleasant two mile trip on the open Massey Ferguson and I was very pleased we contented ourselves with merely cutting off the top of the tree which lay in the road: this I pulled to the opposite verge well clear of traffic where it, like the one at Colworth, could be cleared up another day in more benign conditions. By this time the dull grey light had virtually gone and it had started to rain again, making the return two miles even less enjoyable and I was heading directly into the wind along the main road, squinting beneath the downturned brim of my sou'wester at the rather yellow pool of illumination produced by the headlights, sprayed with additional water every time the nearside front wheel passed through a puddle: the luxuries of weatherproof cabs and powerful headlights were still some way in the future for us.

Relieved to get back into the welcome, relative shelter of the rain lashed yard I put the ignition key in the tractor's toolbox, got down, removed the foam seat cushion and put it in the shed, said goodnight to Jack and the others and shook a selection of wet debris from my jacket before climbing into my own Land-Rover to go home. It was not to be: a tree had fallen across the main road at Manor Farm near the south end of the village, luckily without hitting anyone driving past, and had brought traffic to a standstill. I turned round in the road and went back to inform Frank. While he collected Jack I set off yet again on the winch tractor, being overtaken by them before I reached the blockage and, like the Land-Rover, having to drive down the wrong side of the road to get past the increasing queue. It was pitch dark, the wind roared and rain hosed down as we cut up what lay across the road, working by the light of our Land-Rover's headlamps and those of the stationary traffic, very glad the police had arrived to deal with this because we had no fluorescent jackets or flashing orange beacons in those days and rain soaked waxproofs don't show up well on a dull day, let alone a night like this. We threw the lop and small branches into the field the tree so recently stood in, sometimes twice when the wind blew them back at us; the larger limbs I pulled as far onto the verge as possible: as with the others we would do a proper clear-up another day. The roadside fence had been beaten down and we cobbled the wires together in case there was stock in the field: it was too dark to see anything beyond the beams of light. Having done all we reasonably could in the circumstances we pulled our vehicles onto the verge and let the police oversee the dispersal of the built up queues before we departed. On my way back to the yard for what I fervently hoped would be the last time I realised one or two seams on my jacket had begun to leak and there was a clammy, increasingly cold feeling across my shoulders. This was not surprising as no waterproofs other than oilskins could keep the wearer dry indefinitely and as they were easily torn, too fragile to last long in this work we chose the much tougher and somewhat warmer, though slightly less effective alternative: my Barbour had held up well this wild, wet day, but we were both now in need of some dry warmth and in my case hot food as well.

Happily there were no more alarms. I reached home safely and the hurricane blew itself out during the night: by daybreak there was scarcely a breath of wind. As we collected in the yard next morning Frank gave us an initial update on the situation: we already knew full well the day would be spent clearing windfalls. In addition to those we had been called to yesterday there were three in Whiteleaf Plantation, one in Warren Hanger, two near the river which had both fallen through the lime mortared flint park wall, creating a big repair job for the Buildings Department, and no less than thirty nine between St Roches and Seven Points, of which thirteen blocked the narrow lane. This turned out to be only the tip of a very large wooden iceberg and our day of windfalling became, with interruptions to do pressing 'normal' jobs several months long as more and more were found across the estate; fallen, lodged in other still standing trees or loosened at their roots and liable to fall at any time, therefore potentially dangerous. A large belt of Douglas fir in the bottom of New Severals was so badly damaged Frank had us clear fell it the following spring.

Often trees blown down break up less than those felled because they fall rather more softly, but some of the victims of this storm lay smashed several deep across each other and the resulting heaps had to be unpicked layer by layer, making for slow and difficult progress. One of these was in Chequers plantation west of the village where I had to climb ten feet up and walk along the topmost tree to head it off, a tricky job in itself but necessary to reduce its length and weight before attempting to cut it free of its torn root plate: this would greatly lessen the likelihood of the butt splitting when I did, because in the awful tangle such a happening would be very dangerous as I would not be able to jump out of the way. Squatting sideways on the trunk I pushed the saw under it and cut upwards as far as possible before it began to pinch the bar. That was the easy bit: now I had to cut downwards. The severed butt would spring up when freed of its top so, still sideways, I sawed with legs half bent to absorb the push and avoid being flung off. With a loud crack the wood parted and the end of the butt sprang up by a foot: I wobbled but stayed on it, having switched the saw off the instant it gave way to ensure if I fell the chain would have stopped moving and would therefore do me far less damage should we make serious contact during a possible rapid descent. Chris reversed the winch tractor as close as possible and clambered over the tangle of limbs and trunks to hand me the C hook and end of the winch rope which I attached to the topless tree before getting down. He took up the strain to prevent the butt striking back when I cut it free of its roots. In these situations it was usual with large trees to push the nose of the bar through the middle of the butt and cut down until the timber began to close on it, then saw upwards leaving a small piece uncut: this was a very effective way of avoiding a split butt. The saw was then withdrawn and touched against the top of this uncut piece. I went through this procedure and with a sudden jerk the detached butt instantly rose a couple of feet, at the same time rolling a quarter turn, but it didn't slip back: the moor, freed of the great leverage, fell back with a soft 'flump' and a flurry of disturbed leaves.

Returning to the main road at Manor Farm we had to deal with the two trees down, not one as we thought when clearing the road. The second had fallen at a right angle to the first and we may have failed to notice it in the dark, or it could have blown down later because the storm continued for several more hours. Its top lay like a torn shroud over the moor of the other and would have to be dealt with first. Having lit a fire to burn the twiggery and broken fragments we cut and cleared the tangle of limbs, stacking up everything of cordwood size then decided to roll the butt with the winch to give us space to work on the one whose top had blocked the road: attempting to do so almost resulted in a nasty accident, or worse. A heavy chain was looped round the butt and the C hook attached so that a pull with the winch would cause it to roll, but having put on more strain than should have been required to achieve the desired result it didn't move. We normally stood on one footrest facing the tree if possible when winching, as it was easier to operate the controls and to jump off the tractor if something went wrong, but on this occasion I had no time to do so. The winch rope sang, stretched and parted, the strain suddenly released threw its now detached eye and the heavy C hook twenty yards across the field, past the tractor before I had time to do more than blink and it hit the soft ground beyond with a powerful muddy thump. Had it struck any of us we would in all probability have been killed, but the mishap produced more surprise and annoyance than shock: we now had an apparently immoveable tree and a useless winch rope to contend with. However, necessity is the mother of invention it is said and we solved the rope problem, temporarily at least, by joining the broken ends with a reef knot, pulling gently on the tree to tighten it. Close investigation of the recalcitrant butt revealed a limb underneath driven into the ground, effectively nailing it down and able to resist anything but the most enormous turning force: to cut this we had to dig a hole around it and carefully saw most of the way through, wiping as much soil as possible off the bark before doing so, though it still took the edge off the saw's cutters in the process. It then rolled very easily and we were able to complete the job without encountering further difficulties, finishing by pulling out the buried stub of branch, which was little more than two feet long, and rebuilding the roadside fence.

West's Sawmill in Midhurst bought most of the fallen timber and the cordwood was sold to anyone wanting firewood: there was a great deal of both. What for the first day or two had been a novelty soon became monotonous, the end nowhere in sight and I'm sure Frank was far from overjoyed at the lengthy, unexpected interruption to our schedule. However, I could not help feeling an undeniable sense of pride and satisfaction looking at the neat results of our labours as we finished clearing up each site, some having proved difficult and occasionally dangerous to do. There was also relief in knowing that every one done was one nearer the end, though we were still dealing with the casualties of this storm, between other jobs for the best part of two years!.

CHAPTER 10

CHANGES AFOOT

Arthur retired in 1973 and Frank, his replacement, became an active new broom, ushering in a time of great change. He split us into two gangs, Jack's and Snowy's, which undoubtedly improved productivity as both operated independently and required the purchase of a second Land-Rover. This was followed by the arrival of a Forwarder in December, an extensively modified Ford 5000 tractor fitted with half tracks, a hiab timber crane mounted on top of its heavily redesigned and reinforced cab and a trailer built to handle eight ton loads, the combination costing £6000, which seemed to us a vast amount of money. Bert, from Snowy's gang, was the only one willing to become its driver: Chris and me both refusing as we didn't wish to be stuck on it day after day. There is no doubt it saved a huge number of man hours and an enormous amount of heavy lifting for us, but I felt less than a hundred percent in favour of it because I actually enjoyed the activity: no more would I be expected to lift twenty tons of Bowaters in a day because most of the hauling and lorry loading could now be done by the new machine and the pulling of six levers, though my back would undoubtedly have disagreed. Further evidence of the unstoppable advance of progress and specialisation manifested itself in the middle of August 1974.

Everyone except Jack and Snowy piled out of the Land-Rovers as soon as they stopped in the yard at knocking off time: only they appeared able to contain their curiosity for a few minutes. 'It' had arrived and was standing large and gleaming red beside our own vehicles; a brand new County Skidder with four big wheels, a log rolling blade at the front, double drum winches mounted high on its rear end above a great steel bump plate from which were hanging six choker chains. Perforated armour plating protected its vitals; it had a windscreen and small safety cab but no doors, the side and rear windows being merely strong steel mesh, in fact it was almost an exact replica of the one I had driven briefly at Newton Rigg. We were all over it like a rash, walking round and round, peering underneath to appreciate its generous ground clearance. I had more reason than the others to check it out because Frank had already informed me I was to be its only driver. While this news didn't fill me with gloom in the way the prospect of being forwarder driver did and in some respects was exciting, I could not suppress a slight feeling of disappointment but felt unable to refuse as I had with the forwarder: from now on, whenever we did any timber felling I would be spending my time pulling trimmed out butts to the nearest loading area, not getting further opportunities to fell large trees which I thoroughly enjoyed. Frank appeared, from where I had no idea, and I suggested having an hour or two of practice with it the next day, Saturday, in order to be at least a little familiar with its operation before Monday, when I was expected to use it for the first time in our joint new role.

Eight o'clock in the morning found me in the yard giving it the once over, operator's manual in one hand, before driving up and down a couple of times: it smelled of fresh paint, not diesel, oil and wood. Nothing fell off or sounded to be in mechanical torment so I topped up the fuel tank, put a spade in the cab and ventured onto the main road, heading for the far end of Warren Hanger where we were currently felling. Going downhill to the Selsey Arms I put my hand out as usual to warn motorists I intended turning right onto the Motor Road before remembering it had indicators, a novelty, but by then it was too late to use them. Power steering took all the effort out of swinging the big front wheels round, which was just as well: its steering wheel was a smaller diameter than any of those on the old tractors. The turning

The Skidder

circle however left much to be desired. Having four equally sized wheels and a relatively short wheelbase made it feel very bouncy and it jiggled jauntily over comparatively small undulations in the road, while its eight foot width left little room to spare in the narrow lane to pass any oncoming vehicles I might meet.

Arriving at Warren Hanger I thought it sensible to discover the extent of its hill climbing ability before trying to move any timber. Selecting a clear route from the bottom track to the ride some way up the slope I slipped it into second low, releasing the clutch as I opened the hand throttle wide, and placed my right heel back on the diff lock pedal. Away we went, climbing in fine style, but as the gradient increased engine revs began to drop, quickly becoming laboured and with a stall looking inevitable there was no option but to stamp on the clutch and brakes as I pulled up the handbrake. It stopped instantly with the engine racing, rocking alarmingly fore and aft: for a second I thought it was going to topple backwards, which would have been at least highly embarrassing, certainly painful and potentially fatal. It didn't and I quickly pushed the throttle back to tickover, sitting still for a few moments while a wave of relief flooded over me. I felt sure it had been a narrow squeak, though it was almost certainly a great deal more stable than it felt or the company would not have been selling them. Recovering my shaken composure I contemplated the two options now available: select low reverse and ease it back to flatter ground for another go or put it in first forward and try to continue to the upper ride. The former seemed most sensible: it would probably stall as soon as I lifted the clutch pedal or sit there digging four holes with its tyres if I tried a standing start on the slope and I let it trundle slowly down, the engine revving as it held the weight. Back safely at the bottom it received a mental black mark: power was obviously not its strongest point. To do the job effectively it had to be capable of climbing and descending such slopes with comparative ease. Putting it into low first I opened the throttle as wide as it would go and set off for a second attempt. Once again the engine began to strain as the slope became steeper, but it maintained enough revs to continue pulling and passed the apex of my first go, tyres scrabbling slightly as it clawed the last few yards to the ride with me leaning forward in a totally futile attempt to keep weight on the front end: I weighed ten and a half stone and the tractor at least six tons! However, it certainly was not short of grip.

Having finally conquered the slope I took the easy way down, driving along the ride until it curved downhill to join the bottom track. There was no doubt it would go down any slope it could climb and I turned my attention to the rear end, the new type of winches resembling nothing so much as two cotton reels, their ropes mere string compared to the one on the old, much loved winch tractor which was soon to be sold. Though each of the new winches was rated at four tons safe working load the two tractors were not interchangeable and on many occasions the Massey Ferguson was sorely missed. I soon discovered it required a lot of twisting round in the seat to operate these winches effectively as they had two levers each, a friction clutch and brake which had to be used in a similar manner to those pedals in a car, thus needing both hands working together: it was very hard on my neck. Reversing up to a butt I pulled on the handbrake, put the gear lever into neutral, half turned in the seat and released one winch brake before jumping down to pull out the rope. Lifting one of the choke chains from its notch on the butt plate I looped it round the timber and slipped its free end into the slot in one of the choker eyes on the rope then climbed back into the cab. Twisting round again in the seat to reach the levers I pulled on the clutch, the rope reeling in without any need to rev the engine beyond its steady tickover, picking up the end of the butt. As it rose and bumped against the back plate I pulled the brake on, letting go of the clutch lever at the same time. Simple; it worked a treat.

For more than an hour I practised; pulling timber, bulldozing butts neatly side by side with the blade in the loading area and testing the slope again in reverse. It failed to climb more than halfway up due to the fact that tractor tyres are designed to grip best and be self cleaning only when going forward: as soon as the deep treads filled with earth they were little better than racing slicks and it came to a scrabbling halt with one wheel spinning on each axle as I hadn't bothered to engage the diff lock. I was starting to believe it would prove to be a useful acquisition, though still concerned at the lack of horsepower because it was very heavy. One other drawback manifested itself as I drove out onto the road to return to the yard: the large tyres had picked up a great deal of mud and I was glad of the spade stowed in the cab to scrape up the most obvious lumps they threw off as it gathered speed, having pulled onto the narrow verge to walk back and clear them up. A curate's egg of a machine was my verdict which was to provide both highs and lows as it was asked to flex its muscles in a variety of situations, frustratingly often showing itself to be something of a sheep in wolf's clothing, though to be fair some of its apparent failings resulted from being asked to do things it was never designed for.

I drove it for several months, the initial excitement quickly dissipating and mentally cursing it more often than singing its praises. I was disappointed at its inability to do everything I thought reasonable to ask of it, which occasionally caused us some aggravation, and became thoroughly fed up with the monotony. More than once I had to ask the hauliers taking timber away to West's sawmill to move the largest butts for me with their wonderful old ex-wartime Matador crane lorry because the tractor simply could not budge them. Finally, I asked Frank if I could be taken off it and return to being a woodman. The job was becoming 'not what it was'. It changed a bit more in September 1977 when Jack retired and I became a foreman, finding myself leading what was now the third gang and given most of the big felling work, though we still did many other things. This gave me plenty of opportunity to appreciate, more often despair of, the Skidder from a different perspective: I was no longer its driver but frequently found my plans going awry because it seemed to break down regularly for one reason or another and bits would fall off with depressing frequency, holding up our progress. Frank also left this year and Ian, who had been working closely him for some time, became the new forester.

Chapter II
Goodbye to the coppices

Until the 1970s the estate retained large areas of coppice wood, predominantly hazel with oak standards, though other species of tree and shrub grew in them. The market for hazel products such as thatching spars and pea and bean sticks had been declining for a great many years and almost ceased to exist: the coppices were no longer economic by any stretch of the imagination. To me however their tangled, unkempt wildness, where deer could move unseen, many birds nested and it was possible to become quite disoriented was magical: they supported a huge variety of wildlife. One such compartment boasted a colony of wild daffodils; there were early purple, spotted and butterfly orchids, primroses, many fungi, lichens on the old trees and so much more. It came as most unpleasant news to learn that we would begin clearing them, replanting with a commercial mixture of softwoods and beech following spraying of the hazel stools to prevent their regrowth. I spent many hours exploring these neglected woody treasures and looked upon them as more important than money or the plantations alongside, though with no responsibility for running the estate and keeping its financial head above water I could afford to feel this way. The clearing was in no way thoughtless destruction by uncaring management, but an inevitable result of economic necessity and I like to think I played a very small part in the decision to retain the most important pieces, having spoken more than once to the agent about them. Thirty acres including the glorious wild daffodil colony were leased to Sussex Wildlife Trust, becoming West Dean Woods Nature Reserve, and I was asked to be a member of the management committee. Several other patches were allowed to escape the bite of our chainsaws including seven acres in Stubbs Copse which was rented to Butser Iron Age farm to supply hazel rods for fencing and roundhouse construction. It did nonetheless bring about a huge change in the appearance of parts of the estate and undoubtedly impoverished it ecologically, much being lost without ever being known about or identified.

The hazel stools, not being cut for many years, had become as a result of age and deer browsing gnarled, multi-stemmed spreading bushes while self sown ash and birch grew through and between them and the oak standards. In places, where the mouldering remains of oak tops and accompanying stumps told of past felling from which decay had long since stripped bark and sapwood, they formed groves of mostly clean, straight poles, their symmetry marred here and there by an ash which had grown almost horizontally for a few feet before becoming abruptly vertical: evidence they pre-dated the felling as they must have been saplings when the big trees were cut, pushed over by their great falling tops and the woodmen had not cut them off.

Oak is a light demanding species and grown among coppice produces only short, clean butts: it wants naturally to branch and does so above the shrubby canopy of hazel, the trees in past times being highly valued as the raw material for building timber framed houses and 'the wooden walls of England', the great warships with which for many years Britain really did rule the waves. Now they had become, like the hazel, a waste of potentially profitable space and most had to go.

Though I was saddened by the big clearances much of the work involved was very enjoyable, not least because it provided great variety. Here and there a hazel stool still bore a few straight, clean rods suitable for making bean sticks: these we cut with billhooks to seven feet and tied in bundles of twenty five. They and an equally small quantity of pea sticks picked out from the straightest fine twiggery were taken to the estate gardens or sold for small money to the employees to use in their own vegetable patches. Two metre lengths were cut from the ash poles and sold for making handles, which we called sports ash while the birches were sawn into six foot six inch lengths for turnery and all the rough pieces into four foots for either cordwood or Bowaters, the latter going to the pulp mill in Sittingbourne. These varying lengths were decided not by us but cut to meet the requirements of factories the wood was destined for and four feet was the standard length for cordwood. Any good oak butts free from shake and rot were sold, the rest taken to the estate sawmill and turned into fencing material, gateposts, rails and suchlike while the crooked limbs were of use only as cordwood. Bowater would not take oak because it was no good for pulping and after being stacked along ride edges for a year or two – oak being very slow to season, particularly in the round with its bark on actually requires many years to fully air dry – it was logged and sold for firewood, though often still more or less green and sap filled except at the ends.

There was a large amount of material with no potential use and this we burned, lighting new fires every forty yards or so as we progressed to avoid having to drag this waste too far and aiming the trees towards them wherever possible for the same reason. Hazel twiggery, all the lop and top from the trees plus copious dead wood was consigned to the flames and in the depths of winter, as we progressed slowly like a line of small combines in a harvest field continually cutting down our shelter from cold winds, these were looked upon with great pleasure. A carefully sited one made a far more congenial breaktime companion than the bare aluminium interior of a Land-Rover, though often it was only possible to sit at one side to avoid being pickled by smoke. Robins were constant companions, flying down whenever opportunity offered to forage among the debris, occasionally hopping to the very edge of a fire to snatch some edible morsel before the flames reached it: I have no doubt we burned many thousands of hibernating small creatures. The felled areas looked very neat, with wood stacks of varying sizes in slightly wobbly lines across them, almost regularly spaced grey scars of burned out fires pock marked by the hoofprints of deer which had come to lick at the ash and a wide scatter of the best oak or maiden ash left standing to become future timber. When all the produce had been hauled away the ground was almost completely bare, marked here and there by tractor tyres and ideal for planting up, but sadly quiet, only the stumps left as memorials to what had been lost to progress and changing market demands.

Light flooding the previously heavily shaded earth awoke dormant primroses, violets and in places bluebells, giving them the strength to flower in profusion the second spring after the clearance took place. They had no doubt responded in the same manner every time the wood was coppiced, but for most this would be their final show of exuberance: in a few years ever increasing shade from spreading bramble and the growing trees would send them to a sleep far longer than any previously experienced: it would be a matter of chance whether plant or seed could survive a potential century or more without feeling the sun's warmth.

To speed up the work and reduce the regrowth of hazel, obviating the need for follow-up spraying, when we cleared a section of Stubbs Copse I was told we had to use the Skidder to remove the stools, pulling them out of the ground, roots and all then pushing them onto large fires: particularly stubborn or large ones Mike pummelled first with the dozer blade to loosen their grip. Being there with my gang to fell the trees while this took place close by felt rather like being present at an assault, particularly as we began the job in July, when some birds would still have dependent young in nests: I felt strongly that we were not treating the wood with respect, wasting material which could have provided warmth in our homes, and the ground ended up looking as if it had been on the receiving end of a heavy artillery barrage, with wide, shallow craters and spreads of soil everywhere. Many of the torn rootplates retained a lot of earth and much of this found its way onto the funeral pyres as well: after a day of two they resembled nothing so much as Bronze Age tumuli with smoke emanating from various points, the graves not of important people but an ancient form of woodland management and the wildlife adapted to it. When the clearing was finished and the fires died Mike spread the mounds of accumulated soil, uncovering unburned wood, scorched lumps and masses of charcoal, some pieces as thick and long as our arms: he had almost and completely unintentionally recreated old time earth covered charcoal kilns.

Having been somewhat reluctantly in charge of this particular piece of destruction, I was not surprised when my gang were then given the job of rabbit fencing the compartment before it was planted. One morning, while taking us and some stakes to where we had knocked off the previous day, driving along what was marked out as a new ride through the middle, the Land-Rover stopped with a loud thump and the engine stalled as I hit an unseen obstacle, jolting us all forward. From behind me, when they had recovered their composure came a variety of ribald comments about my driving and I joined in the merriment before restarting, reversing and steering round what we discovered to be a stump almost hidden beneath loose earth, giving it no more thought. Only weeks later, when the vehicle was taken to Brickkiln for a service did Bob discover the damage: the impact had broken one end of the gearbox crossmember off the chassis! This would probably not have happened had we carried out the clearance by hand as before because there would have been no mound of earth dragged against the offending stump to hide it. I couldn't help thinking this must have been a last despairing gesture of defiance from the poor wrecked wood.

CHAPTER 12
AFFAIRS OF THE HEART

Occasionally we drove past the long, elegant flint façade of West Dean College if we were working in the park and once or twice some of us had been drafted in to help clear out decades of accumulated stuff from rooms that were to be redecorated and become accommodation or classrooms as its activities and international reputation increased: much of this was rubbish, but it grieved me to see thrown away items which had some historical interest; boxes of old glass plate negatives and moth eaten mounted heads of African animals among them. Some of us became members of the college social club, able to buy drinks at the bar which was built at one side of the great hall; we saw students come and go, heard various snippets of gossip but were more or less completely in the dark as to what happened there on a daily basis and this meant we felt divorced from it, creating a tangible them and us attitude.

In an attempt to overcome this, on June 2nd 1976 the college held an open day, when the other departments could visit and have a good look round: we were given an afternoon off to go, free to enter any of the classes, talk to students and tutors and gain a better understanding of its work. We returned the courtesy later with Land Rover and tractor tours of the estate. With several other woodies I went into the bookbinding workshop where a small number of students were hard at work, one having something explained to him by their tutor.

They stopped and spoke to us as our questions flowed, but my eyes were drawn as if by magnetism to a slim, raven haired figure seated on the opposite side of the room with her back to the door, involved in what appeared to be a delicate task. She continued for a short while then apparently reached a point where the project could safely be left and turned to join in the conversation. I found myself gazing at the most beautiful girl I had ever seen. My heart leapt and all interest in the college, bookbinding, the woods, everything instantly faded to insignificance. For a few minutes more we chatted with the group before moving on to the next class, but a vision of her lovely oriental face remained with me and my one thought for the rest of the day was how could I see her again and have an opportunity to talk to her. Not until I lay in bed on the verge of sleep did an idea come to me: there was an 1838 volume of Colonel Peter Hawker's Instructions to Young Sportsmen on my bookshelf which had at some time been rather crudely rebound with thick orange brown leather: it was a sturdy piece of restoration, but far from professional and would serve as the perfect excuse for returning to the college next evening.

She was my first thought on waking, indeed the only one of any importance. The working day dragged: every hour seemed endless, as if the hands of my watch were having to push their way through treacle and I also had to make my weekly squirrel hopper round afterwards, checking and topping them up where necessary. I confess to driving round the Windens, Phyllis Wood and Hooksway as though in a cross country rally, the book wrapped in a bag on the Land-Rover's seat beside me, stamping on the brakes and running from the vehicle to look at each hopper as I came to it: I was back at the college soon after most of the classes had eaten their evening meal. Walking into the bar I halfheartedly asked for a beer and sipped it with no sense of enjoyment. Across the other side of the room sat the girl, relaxed and chatting to another student, a long dress accentuating her delightful figure. I yearned to go over and speak to her but could not summon up the courage, merely waiting impotently for what seemed an interminably long time until she left, to return to her class I desperately hoped.

After delaying impatiently a few more minutes I went down to the bookbinding room and there she was, busy at her table once more, as were several other students. I spoke to the tutor and showed him the book, knowing I could probably never justify the cost of having a professional rebinding job done on it, but it was only a smokescreen for my return visit in any case. A cheerful conversation developed in which she took an active part and some of my remarks caused general merriment; her smiling face, sparkling dark eyes and gentle American accent twisting my stomach into knots of delight and desperation. I stayed until the students decided they had done enough for the day and began leaving, timing my own departure to be just in front of her. As we left the room I turned, screwed up my courage and asked if I could see her tomorrow. She suggested I join her for lunch in the college, her last because she was returning to London later in the afternoon to attend a calligraphy course when this one ended and then going back to America. My hopes and my heart were dashed to the floor: there was no possible way I could do so because we were working several miles away and I couldn't take what would amount to half a day off from our job without prior notice unless illness struck, however much I wanted to, and I could hardly claim to be ill then appear in the college. It was to be hello and goodbye. I smiled and wished her good luck for the next course and her journey, said goodnight and went home feeling utterly wretched. Gradually the feeling diminished but an awful emptiness remained: in those brief moments she made an indelible mark in my heart and had taken a small part of me with her.

We were thinning in Birch Copse on the 25th, another boiling hot day in what was to become a record summer and by mid-morning my saw began coughing, spluttering and refusing to run. I swept the Land-Rover's tailboard clean with my forearm before beginning to dismantle the carb on it, expecting to find a speck of dirt in one of the jets, but there was nothing obvious and finally it refused to start at all. As there were no spare saws I drove back to West Dean, found Frank in the estate office and asked him what was to be done. He decided I should take it to our saw dealer near Haslemere and ask him to sort out the problem, handing me a letter as I left which I put without looking at in my lunchbag on getting back to the vehicle, wondering idly why the estate were writing to me. It was almost as hot driving with the windows and bulkhead ventilators wide open as it had been in the woods and I decided to stop for dinner beside the long, stoney track which led from the outskirts of the town to Michael Richmond's small base in a large shed at the end of his garden way up in the woods, putting my right boot in such a position it held the door open. The forgotten letter fell out as I picked up my sandwich box.

It wasn't the kind of envelope the office normally used and the address mystified me: written in a very neat hand were the words "To, the auburn haired man with a beard who I think works in the Forestry Department." My puzzlement turned to overwhelming joy as I opened it and took out the single page it contained. It was a letter from Elizabeth, the girl on the bookbinding course: she was still in London and could come down the next weekend! Suddenly the sun shone even more brightly and my heart sang with delight: the gnawing emptiness which had been my constant companion for three weeks vanished as excitement surged through me like an electric shock. I would be seeing her again for two whole days!

The cause of my saw's problem was quickly diagnosed: it was suffering the mechanical equivalent of heat stroke and was not the first to be brought in with similar symptoms during this very hot spell. There was a relief valve in the petrol tank which should vent excess pressure build up in very hot conditions, but it had ceased to work properly and too much fuel was being forced into the crankcase, effectively flooding it. Having cleaned it out, dried the wet spark plug and replaced the faulty valve Michael started the saw and it ran like a dream. I remember nothing of my drive back to Birch Copse, but even now wonder if the others noticed any change in my demeanour: though I tried hard to conceal it I felt as if I was walking on air.

Those two days were an exquisite agony: we walked and talked, ate lunch in a pub; I drove her to Bignor Roman Villa, which unfortunately was closed and back through the villages below the north face of the Downs. She held out her hand and I took it in mine, another electric shock surging through me at the touch of her soft olive skin against my calloused fingers. I loved her. I was brimming with love for her but, like a fractured dam holding back all but a few drops of the torrent because she said "Please don't fall in love with me," and when I asked why answered "Because I'll break your heart." I knew, if I told her it was already too late that I would never see her again, an unbearable thought and somehow I held the fracture together, hoping with every fibre of my being that eventually she would feel as I did and the dam could be allowed to burst.

Shortly after I departed the woods temporarily for my long planned ten week visit to Papua New Guinea, a trip of a lifetime. My only regret was that Elizabeth was thousands of miles away in America. I wrote long letters, received some in return and sent her a brilliantly coloured 'meri dress' as a present, a kind of long, loose blouse most local women wore in which she would look even more beautiful I thought. I told her of all my adventures, described the scenery and the people and continued to yearn for her. The great drought of that summer broke the day before I returned: it had been almost as hot as the tropics when I left, though not so humid, and coming back to normal September weather was a bit of a shock to the system. I looked forward to returning to work and regaling the woodies with tales from the West Pacific, but much more importantly, Elizabeth would be coming to England for another course in London and I would be able to see her again.

We spent two more delightful weekends together; I went to London for a day and she came down for a day, the last time I saw her before she returned to America. On Christmas Day I drove to her London digs and put a card through the door: I knew she would not be in but hoped it would reach her before she left. We wrote to each other and made tentative plans for me to visit her in America, but then her letters became less frequent, the final one containing the news I most feared and dreaded hearing: she had fallen in love with someone in New York and would not be returning to England. I sat for a long time in turmoil: my heart telling me to catch the first available plane to America and not give in without a fight, while my head said our lives and lifestyles were so completely different the gap was insurmountable and I could not bear the thought that by going I would probably succeed only in making her hate me. A few days later I sent her my very best wishes and hope to this day she is enjoying a blissfully happy life.

To behave normally when every moment my thoughts were elsewhere and my spirit inhabited a lonely, dark place was extremely difficult. I was still empty inside when, in the evening of July 3rd 1977, after a day spent wardening at Kingley Vale I walked round the park, looking with little enthusiasm for the barn owls I knew lived in the vicinity and stopped off at the college for a drink before going home. It was a means of passing a few minutes but I wasn't trying to drown my sorrows. As I reached the bar a very attractive, dark haired girl came up and asked if I could be the person she had seen momentarily on the reserve that afternoon. She was attending a silversmithing course in the college and spent the weekend with a Conservation Corps group working on the new dewpond in the valley. I had been standing outside the reserve's small museum when their Land-Rover went past and had probably seen her as I glanced briefly down at the dozen human ants toiling in the sun way below while I walked, lost in sad thoughts on the hill. A shaft of bright light speared into my black world as if a door had suddenly opened to let the sun shine in: this was my introduction to Charlotte.

I bought her a drink, we chatted and I asked her for a date: on a warm evening the following week I took her to Old Severals to see the nightjars which were nesting in the area we had clear felled the previous winter. She never told me that she didn't know what a nightjar was when we set off and it never occurred to me that asking her get into my Land-Rover through the driver's door because the passenger one was tied shut due to the catch having broken might make her a little uneasy about my motives. We stood quietly, listening to the wonderful mechanical churring of the male, a magical sound of summer and saw him flying about while dusk crept across the land, as light and fluttering as a butterfly: his reeling song filling the sweet scented air and the lovely girl by my side making it a very special evening. I decided then to ask her for another date when I dropped her back at the college and she said yes! We walked for miles and at the top of Lodge Hill she admitted not remembering my name, a momentary blow to my confidence but our joint merriment at her confession quickly dispelled my fears.

Her course finished at the end of the week and she returned to her job and shared house in London, but a small voice inside told me this time I had no need to worry. The following weekend she returned, to stay with me at Hog's Common: we got on like a house afire and I felt we already shared something more than friendship. Over the next three months I waited impatiently on Friday evenings to hear the sound of her mini clubman estate arriving, though sometimes she went to visit her parents in Cheshire and I spent a couple of weekends in London: being met at Richmond and having to keep up with her little green car as she led me to Stockwell called for a driving technique totally alien to the poor old Land-Rover, whose tyres had never before come even close to squealing on a roundabout. I showed her many of my favourite places and was delighted that she willingly rolled up her sleeves and immersed herself in my world. We phoned and wrote letters, went to the West Country for a camping holiday and she helped me in the garden: gazing at her crouched by the vegetable plot produced the most intensely pleasurable tingle through my body and she became an ever more important part of my life, so much so that by October I knew she was the girl I wished to spend the rest of my days with. On the 23rd I asked her if she would marry me and she said yes!!! Our blossoming love had given my life new purpose: even the most mundane work no longer felt such a chore because the dark cloud of depression which had affected everything I did since that final letter from America had been swept away. I felt as joyful as the skylark rising into a blue spring sky to sing his heart out: the world had once more become a happy place.

The college continues teaching and still has little direct, day to day contact with the rest of the estate so far as I can glean from those members of my family living nearby, but I have so very much to thank it for: without its unintentional help I would never have met my life partner.

Chapter 13
Squirrel Poisoning

Though we enjoyed a good day's squirrel poking we always knew the activity did nothing to solve the problem of bark stripping: only a concerted and sustained effort across the entire country, in town and city as well, to kill every grey squirrel seen would stand any hope of effectively reducing their numbers and the loss of quality timber production their activities were responsible for. This was unlikely ever to happen and in some parts of the country estates had virtually given up trying to grow beech or sycamore timber. A more effective means of dealing with them was introduced – poison. No-one liked the idea of using this, but it had the undeniable advantage of effectively reducing their numbers during the critical period – May to July – when the stripping takes place. Warfarin was the only poison allowed to be used: it was considered a comparatively humane one as it prevents blood clotting and victims 'painlessly' bleed to death because even the most robust squirrels would have small scratches at some point in their digestive tract. We were told it had to be eaten on four consecutive days to be effective. Legislation governing its use stipulated that the poison had to be administered only on whole wheat grains placed in approved L-shaped hoppers designed to prevent other animals and birds from gaining access and they could not be used in any part of the country where red squirrels still occurred. The warfarin came in bottles and contained a deep maroon dye so that treated wheat could easily be recognised and not fed by accident to livestock. Each bottle contained the correct amount to treat twenty eight pounds of wheat: we weighed this out in plastic sacks, checked carefully for leaks beforehand and tipped the contents of a bottle into each one, giving them a good shaking round to ensure every grain was covered then putting them aside to dry.

It was recommended that to have maximum effect hoppers should be put out at a density far greater than was practical for us: setting them out and checking each one regularly would have been virtually a full time job. We decided it would be possible only to ensure they were evenly spread and known hotspots were covered, making weekly visits to top them up. This became an overtime job for three of us and I took on the park area, transferring a couple of years later to the woods west of Sandy's Bottom which had added convenience from 1977 when I moved to Hog's Common, only a stone's throw from the Bottom. I made my first round at the end of April, the Land-Rover loaded with hoppers, sacks of treated grain and another of whole maize which was to be used as bait to draw squirrels to them. I topped the load off with a chainsaw, having filled it up with fuel and chain oil in case there were any rides blocked by fallen trees: my planned route would take me along many of the narrow, rarely used rides where a tree could fall and not be discovered for months. Even without any such hitches there was no hope of covering the entire beat in three hours as I had to seek out likely places to put each hopper where squirrels would find them, but they would not be obvious to anyone intent on mischief: it took me all this time to go round Phyllis Wood and Stubbs Copse and the rest would have to wait until the following week. It had been a bright and breezy day and felt very pleasant jolting slowly along the rutted rides, stopping every so often to site a hopper, the setting sun visible through the trees and the air softly fragrant, vibrant with the birds' evening chorus. As far as possible I put them between the roots of trees so they were fairly well hidden and less likely to be knocked about by inquisitive deer: we had more than one robbed by them. The first I put by a tall Douglas fir, tucked well into a crevice between two large roots and filled it with wheat, having first given the bag a good shake to make sure the warfarin coated grains were not stuck together and would flow into the narrow slot at the back of the horizontal tunnel part. This done I scattered maize for several yards around, more thickly close to it: the large yellow grains would undoubtedly soon be found, and not only by squirrels. To make sure they learned where the hopper was this prebaiting might have to be repeated for the following couple of weeks. That done I climbed back into the vehicle and closed the door as quietly as is possible in a Land-Rover devoid of soundproofing or internal trim, noting the location on a large scale map so I didn't forget and ensure that if for some reason I was unable to do the round my stand-in would be able to find it. Starting the engine and moving the long gearstick into first I drove on, only to see a roe doe bound across the ride fifty yards in front, her neck already looking a little ragged as the long winter hair had begun falling out: soon she would become bright foxy red in her summer pelage. I stopped to watch her but she ran on out of sight, obviously suspicious but not sufficiently alarmed to bark.

Driving on I found the ride completely blocked by a fallen birch; quite a large spready one which had come down across a wet patch greened in parts by moss. I put on my safety helmet, snapped down the earmuffs and took the saw out, drop starting it as I walked to the tree: while there was no standing water the moss free mud still glistened and my boots sank two inches into it. The blare of the saw shattered the evening peace and I was glad it didn't take more than a couple of minutes to cut the tree up: there was no point doing a thorough job and trimming it out properly as it would never be collected; I merely cut it into pieces small enough to manhandle from the ride before switching off the motor and restoring tranquility to the woods. Most of the limbs I dragged to the ride edge, leaving scores of shallow scars across the mud and tearing ragged grooves in the moss carpets, upending the pieces of butt which were too heavy to carry and getting my hands coated with mud in the process: I wiped off the worst on a nearby tree then finished the job by rubbing them up and down my thighs.

There were no more obstacles to delay me but sunset was a fast fading pink blush staining the south western horizon and dusk had begun to fill the woods before I put out the last hopper. The light breeze had died away completely and darkness slowly congealed the now motionless spring scented air, enveloping the trees in its soft indigo cloak: above the first stars began to twinkle faintly. My fingers touched the light switch but I decided not to turn them on and destroy the scene with shafts of man made illumination: enough light remained for me to drive carefully the half mile out of the woods and back to the public road where I would legally and necessarily need their help to return home safely.

In spring 1978 I was able sometimes to have Charlotte's company on my evening round, which added immensely to the pleasure of being in the woods. On one occasion her feminine muscle came in extremely useful when the Land-Rover refused to start after I had stopped to refill a hopper in Stoney Dale plantation: we had to push it to where the track went down into the Dale itself and I could bump start it. A similar thing happened on another evening in the same place with the same Land-Rover, but this time I was alone. The pushing was so much harder!

While the hoppers proved extremely effective in killing squirrels when it was most necessary to do so and thereby reducing barking damage to a tiny fraction of previous levels, they were not entirely successful in preventing other species from gaining access to the poison. There was genuine concern over the possibility of secondary poisoning as a result of victims being found and eaten. We very rarely found a dead squirrel and assumed they usually died in their dreys, but some may well have been picked up by foxes. Dead or dying woodmice were occasionally discovered close to hoppers, but if it was true that a good dose had to be taken in on four consecutive days to effect its lethal work our concern may well have been largely unnecessary, except for the unfortunate mice. However, it was not unusual to find golden pheasants dead in the tunnels: being smaller than ordinary pheasants they were able to push themselves in to reach the grain, but their feet could get no purchase to pull themselves out again. As it was only necessary to check and top up hoppers once a week their bodies could be very ripe by the time they were found and they had in the meantime rendered them useless for their intended job, probably themselves suffering a death much worse than poisoning.

CHAPTER 14
THE RIVERSIDE CLUMP

John, one of the gamekeepers, lived at the bottom of the village in a cottage close by the little River Lavant which meanders though the estate, and on the opposite side a short way downstream stands another which was occupied by a farmworker and his family: they are both situated little higher than the stream banks and therefore vulnerable to winter floods. A winterbourne, its flow ceased in spring and didn't resume some years until well into winter: throughout summer and autumn its stony bed was dry and covered with a fine layer of silt, but in February 1978 there was a good flow of water, in those days almost certainly tainted by pollution from the adjoining dairy farm. Beside John's cottage stood a clump of dead and dying trees which had to be cut down and a pen in which he kept geese, ducks, guineafowl and chickens. His garden was separated from the park fields by a substantial but very rusty iron fence which in grander times would probably have been painted black. This had to be taken out in order that the timber and cordwood could be hauled away and to give us a bit more space, though we wanted to keep all the lop and top in as small an area as possible to make clearing up easier. Old and rusty it may have been, but it was still sturdy and we had to break it into manageable sections by dismantling the original pinned joints with a hammer and cold chisel before we were able to prise its double spiked feet out of the ground with a crowbar and remove it: only then could we start work on the trees.

They were a mixture of sycamore, elm and beech, some so dead they had begun dropping limbs and had to be felled without damaging John's cottage, his pen, and for our own comfort not dropped into the river: space was therefore rather limited. Starting my saw caused some initial consternation among the confined birds, but they soon became used to the noise of our activities and appeared to look on us as a source of entertainment, brightening their otherwise humdrum days. First to come down was a sycamore, a sizeable and very dead double stemmed tree which held together until it hit the ground, the impact causing both trunks to break into several large pieces. It didn't take us long to clear up: the dry twigs and small branches very soon becoming a welcome, hot fire. The second and what turned out to be last of the day was a very large, dead beech: this had a big limb on the park side which gave it some back weight as well as making it want to fall into the park field. I needed to fell it within John's garden to keep the area of destruction as small as possible and also avoid a nearby yew which was to be retained, but the working area was so confined we could not get the Skidder in to winch it over: we would have to use a sledgehammer and wedges. Removing the claws and sink took me a few minutes and Mike stood ready to hammer in a wedge as soon as the felling cut was far enough into the butt it wouldn't hit the saw chain. To avoid any tendency of a tree to drop back and pinch the saw, at the same time increasing its back weight and making wedging harder work, it was essential at least one was put in as soon as possible. I could tell from the sound as he struck it the wedge was having no effect in lifting the tree and he hammered in a second with similar results: getting it over was going to be hard work.

Having completed the felling cut, leaving a good hold to ensure it didn't break off and fall sideways into the field or far worse, backwards onto John's cottage, I removed the saw and put it safely out of the way. Taking the hammer from Mike I put in a third wedge which caused the cut to widen only very slightly. We had two more and hammered these in, working towards both sides of the tree to keep the upward force equal as a further precaution against a break-off, knocking out the initial one by striking it on alternate sides until it became loose enough to pull free. More height was needed so we freed a second in the same manner and put the two on top of each other. This didn't work as they kept springing out; their combined angle too broad to drive into the still depressingly narrow cut. Finding a suitable, solid piece of the felled sycamore I sawed out two wooden wedges, thinner than the steel ones, making sure their grain ran along their length for maximum strength and we hammered them in, each with a steel one on top. This proved somewhat more successful and very slowly the cut began to open. A second pair of steel wedges were freed and hammered in on top of each other, happily doing exactly what we intended this time. We had discarded our jackets by now and were breathing heavily from the exertion, yet still the tree refused to fall. We hammered and hammered, slowly working the wedges, wooden and steel, round to the sides and knocking a piece of cordwood I sawed to a wedge shape in at the back to help ensure the hold would not rip out and the tree pivot over the wedges to fall backwards with potentially disastrous results for the cottage, and our future prospects as woodmen. Our faces shone with sweat and the cut widened with infinite slowness until, after a solid fifty five minutes of pounding, it began to fall. The top broke up with a resounding crash as it struck the ground, falling away from the cottage and pen but doing a little damage to the yew because the big limb on the park side caused it to swing slightly to the left of my aiming point. We stood for a short while, exhausted, while Kevin and Tim began the trimming out. Too dead to make timber, we had to turn it all into logs, but not before I measured the butt: it was 288 hoppus feet, quite large for a beech.

Because this job had to be fitted in as and when weather conditions, principally wind, prevented us from timber felling in Church Clump, it took several weeks to complete but eventually, a month later we had only a small handful of trees left to cut and they were all done in one day. There were no problems until we came to the final one, a large sycamore which was growing on the lip of the riverbank, with one corner of John's pen touching it on the other side. To add to the difficulty of getting it down the big saw could not reach through it, forcing me to make part of the felling cut from beside the pen then stand in the river to complete it at shoulder height: in that position the saw felt very heavy and awkward and it was hard on my arms. At least it needed no wedging. It began to lift then fell sideways due to what is known as a 'running hold' – when the grain curves from the back cut into the sink, effectively destroying the hinge. It did no damage to the pen but fell full length into the river, spraying water everywhere except over me, for which I was very grateful. The resulting dam raised the river level six inches almost immediately and I was lucky to scramble up the bank with the saw without getting my boots filled. When the laughter finally subsided we knew there was some urgent work to be done or John and the farmer's family might soon be sweeping water out of their homes. Luckily a lot of the dead limbs had broken up as they hit and we could pick the pieces out of the river, but a few were intact and needed sawing: some contortions were required to avoid being soaked by the chip filled water which sprayed up each time a speeding chain touched the surface. We worked as quickly as possible, cutting, picking up and throwing pieces onto the bank, two-ing those too heavy to lift on our own while maintaining a precarious balance on the half submerged butt: they could be stacked up properly later. By knocking off time we had removed everything except the butt from the river, becoming quite damp in the process. This seemed not to impede the flow very much and the danger of flooding the cottages had been averted. At that point I said farewell to the boys: they could remove it in the morning in whatever manner they chose because I would be driving to Cheshire where Charlotte and I were to be married three days later in her home town of Nantwich. I had been unable to concentrate fully on the job all week, but knew it was the running hold and not a mistake I made which caused the tree to go wrong, therefore didn't feel too bad leaving them to sort out the last bit.

My marriage to Charlotte didn't entirely push aside thoughts of working full time in conservation: every now and then I saw a job advertised which looked interesting and the Nature Conservancy passed on information of posts with other organisations, but nothing came of all but one them. In February 1980 The Society of Sussex

Downsmen were looking for a part time warden to manage their two small reserves, Heyshott Down on the scarp slope of the downs close to the village of that name and the Devil's Jumps, a line of five Bronze Age barrows which have pimpled the crest of Treyford Hill, part of the estate for over four thousand years. The Agent knew several of the Downsmen's management committee members and put my name forward; I had an interview and was offered the post! Charlotte was happy for me to take it, though it would mean spending many weekend days at one or other site: she often came with me and we enjoyed working together with a variable number of volunteers. Later the same month I was appointed assistant forester at the princely sum of £72.50 per week and was still eligible to earn piecework as a top-up. All the extra income was most timely because at the end of October our son was born: we named him Martin after the delightful little house martins, those dolphins of the air ocean which returned each spring to nest under the eaves of our cottage and were such welcome summer guests. Life became extremely busy and could scarcely get any better.

CHAPTER 15
CHIPPING

After a good deal of research it had been decided by the estate's trustees to install a woodburning system to heat the college and provide hot water, while excess heat would be utilised to heat greenhouses in the gardens and some nearby cottages: this was intended to reduce the no doubt enormous sums spent annually on heating oil and electricity and was very forward looking, though undoubtedly an expensive plan. We woodies had no part in any of this, merely witnessing the new boiler house being built and surrounded by a high wall designed to reduce noise levels outside and seeing the trench dug from it across the lawned gardens in which was constructed the insulated hot water supply pipe to the college. This was at the time a relatively new concept and involved trips to France for those charged with buying one essential component of the system, the wood chipper: with two thousand acres of trees across the estate providing fuel would not be a problem, but sourcing a machine sufficiently robust to withstand the enormous strain of reducing pieces of wood up to ten inches in diameter to chips was not a simple matter: trials of various chippers available in this country having proved useless.

We were informed that some of us would be doing the chipping, news which came as little surprise: the department spent its days dealing with wood and moving it about and was, without wishing to blow our trumpet too loudly, the only one able to provide a fit team to operate it on a regular basis. In August 1980 a suitably large chipper was eventually bought and taken to the estate workshop at Brickiln Farm: as purchased it was not powered, the choice of engine being left to the buyer, but needed to be at least a hundred horsepower. Bob, the estate mechanic and previously an engineer in the army, sourced a Bedford lorry chassis with engine and gearbox from Potters, the army surplus dealers whose Aladdin's cave of lorries, Land-Rovers, spares and many other mechanical delights occupied more than a quarter mile of the deceased railway and Singleton station on the edge of the estate: I once saw half an aircraft wing complete with RAF roundel propped against the wall at the station entrance! There were two Alsatian guard dogs kenneled in what had been the station yard with a sign nailed above their accommodation warning visitors – "Beware guard dogs, this one is angry, the other is bloody livid!" It was normal practice when going there to buy spare parts for our vehicles to approach the office with hands firmly in pockets if the dogs were loose as one had the hair raising habit of running soundlessly up from behind and playfully grabbing a shoulder as he passed: shoulders are a bit more robust than fingers!

Bob removed the propshafts, reverse and one forward gear from the box before marrying the chipper to the chassis, leaving three forward gears as its flywheel was so heavy it could only be brought up to full speed gradually in the same manner as the lorry had been in its previous life, but the controls would have to be operated from the ground. The 'some of you' was narrowed as time drew near for its initiation to me and my gang, the sweetener used to drum up our enthusiasm was that they needed workers who would look after it; not that this dubious compliment had much of the desired effect. It was intended to be mobile, to be towed to stacks of timber in the woods and the chips it produced transported by trailer to West Dean. We had to go over to Brickiln where Bob showed us how to operate it and also test a suitable trailer for moving the chips, taking it down to the boiler house and tipping it to ensure it would not hit the roof at full lift, which could only be achieved by putting an extra three and a half gallons of hydraulic oil in the tractor's rear axle, a lot more than was supposed to be there.

The day came for the trial run: it was taken over to Whiteleaf Plantation where we set it in position beside a stack of larch poles, pointing its swivelling chute into the chip trailer and awaiting the arrival of various important people to watch the proceedings. Bob started it and we began pushing the larch into its well guarded feed opening. To the powerful hum of the engine were added loud wooden grinding noises and in moments each pole was ejected as a dense cloud of chips into the trailer, transforming them almost as quickly as we could put them in and impressing everyone. This done and the trailer full we all went over to West Dean to watch it being tipped into the open end of the boiler building: this proved less than entirely satisfactory and produced an immediate change of plan: the chipper would be put in the boiler house yard and wood taken to it. Though chipping in the woods would have been far more pleasant we were very pleased the plan was discarded because it would have created a lot of unnecessary problems, among them blown oil seals in the overfilled tractor. It would be much more efficient to have wood taken to the boiler house and chipped directly into it as we would not have to stand around having filled the trailer, unable to do anything until it returned empty and there had never been plans to have more than one. I had no doubt the wasted time which would have been an inescapable part of this system had not escaped the attention of the decision makers and heavily influenced the outcome.

As with most new items of equipment there was some initial excitement, but this didn't last very long. We had to have another trial run, in the boiler house yard this time attended by further important persons and the local press. It had been brushed down, towed over to West Dean and parked in the yard and stood waiting with its chip chute aimed at the vast empty space comprising half the building. Geoff had hauled in a load of two metre more or less straight cordwood, mostly beech and ash and stacked this neatly close by. Across the floor of the chip store were long, hydraulically operated reciprocating arms, each with a series of wedge shaped protrusions on top which were designed to drag chips to the feed auger, thence to the boiler and we were told these needed to be well covered before they would work properly.

Because it had to be operated from the ground Bob had extensively altered the controls and though all drivers, able to work clutch, gears and accelerator in a car without conscious thought, it took more than our brief introduction at Brickiln and the session in Whiteleaf to become equally familiar at doing so with our hands while standing beside it – pushing down the clutch lever and flicking the throttle with the left hand while changing gear with the right. After making a couple of dummy runs I turned the key and the engine burst into a throaty tickover. Snapping down the earmuffs and visor on my safety helmet I began the procedure, misjudged second gear and had to start again. Success this time and having opened up to full throttle in top gear the combination made a considerable roar, sounding noticeably louder than it had in the woods as the sound reverberated around the walled yard. Kevin took a length of wood from the heap and pushed it in, the blades in the fast spinning flywheel grabbing it and reducing it to chips almost instantly, flinging them over twenty feet from the chute against the back wall of the store with a long 'thwaaack' audible even to us through our earmuffs standing close to the machine. They spilled down and became an insignificant scatter on the pristine concrete floor, the earlier trailer load still forming an untidy heap at the front. The assembled dignitaries proved to be as impressed as those we entertained at Whiteleaf. A larger piece followed and was also chewed up within a very few seconds. We put several more lengths through before the demonstration was declared a complete success and I closed the throttle to slow the great flywheel, putting the gearbox into neutral and turning off the engine: the flywheel continuing to revolve for a while under its own momentum. The agent, college principal, trustees and invited onlookers departed and we were left in peace to put the rest of the load through, some six tons, then wait for Geoff to bring in more wood.

The entire system had to be thoroughly tested and the boiler could only be lit when there were sufficient chips to run it for several days: our demonstration run had produced what looked like a small molehill at the rear of the cavernous space, utterly insignificant compared with the trailer load tipped very untidily at the open front during the morning and attempting to visualise how many loads it would require to satisfy the technicians proved impossible: we could see only that it was going to be several. Starting up again we put one of the largest diameter pieces in, a length of beech so heavy it needed two of us to lift: the engine took up the strain as the chipper made its already familiar loud grinding sound, the exhaust note deepening as a plume of smoke came from the pipe and the 'thwaaack' of chips hitting the wall was slightly extended. It would be fair to say we were a little in awe of its enormous power and already aware that, favoured gang or not, we had been given an extremely heavy and dirty job which would quickly lose its novelty appeal.

It didn't take very long to decide that a bucket chain approach was not the best way to work and we began operating a circular system, picking up a piece each and putting it in the machine one after another but two-ing any very heavy lengths. The chipper gobbled everything in its stride and for our own amusement as much as anything we decided to see if it was possible to overwhelm its huge appetite by increasing the feed rate to the point where there was no gap between the individual lengths, as though it was chipping an endless pole. It coped without complaint, though the engine did slowly lose a few revs and the continuous spray of chips hitting the back wall sounded rather like a distant waterfall. With wood stacked close to the machine we could easily feed faster than its voracious maw could swallow, allowing us brief moments of relaxation between turns.

The stack had been reduced to a few poles when Geoff arrived on the forwarder with another load, giving us no choice but to stop: we couldn't safely pick up pieces while he was unloading onto the same spot and a break was very welcome: it was definitely not a lightweight job. The original six tons of timber had looked a sizeable heap, but as chips in the building that same six tons appeared to have shrunk dramatically: we would need to put through at least two more loads to ensure the quantity was sufficient to cover all the dragging arms when spread with shovels to a more or less even thickness so the boiler test could begin. While Geoff unloaded we took a well earned breather, brushed off our personal accumulations of debris and opened our flasks, wondering if those in the college benefitting from our efforts would feel as warm as we did when any bugs in the system had been ironed out and it was in full operation. Indeed they would: a few weeks later news reached us that temperatures in the offices had climbed to 90 degrees Fahrenheit – in January – and they had been forced to open the windows because the dry heat was starting to shrink and warp the lovely old oak paneling! Some fine tuning was obviously necessary but no-one had any doubt that the set-up was highly efficient.

The chipper produced, in addition to its primary product, clouds of wood dust and bark fragments: having discovered this during the trial runs we put on masks as well as hearing and eye protection, all very necessary but not enjoyed encumbrances. None of this protected our clothes from a head to toe covering of the airborne debris. While Geoff took great care to keep the wood he brought in as clean as possible some lengths, particularly those which had been in contact with the ground were ingrained with mud and even small stones. These we needed to brush off as well as possible to prevent damage to the chipper blades which were expensive and required specialised facilities to resharpen, it was not the sort of job we or even Bob could contemplate doing: they were to be taken to Frazer Nash, an engineering firm in Midhurst which possessed the necessary precision equipment.

When Geoff finished unloading we started chipping again and had disposed of this second load a while before he returned with a third: when all the teething troubles had been ironed out and the system was in full operation he hauled in several loads each week so we could chip for a full day without being held up. After another well earned drink and breather we began to spread out the growing heap of chips in the store with shovels: the air had cleared of dust but possessed a strong aroma of the beech and ash we had so rapidly reduced to pieces not much larger than 50 pence coins, blended here and there with the sweet aroma of the larch from Whiteleaf. Blindfolded I could have told any onlooker which species we were working with: their scents are very characteristic.

As this operation took us away from our primary work, Ian soon decided we would go down once a week, on Fridays, to keep the chip store well filled, which made the weekends very welcome. This plan was far from perfect because the amount of chips used varied as demands for hot water and heating did and I suggested we chip on wet days when otherwise we would be languishing in the pickle yard. Ian knew from his own experience that productivity was very low there and it didn't need most of the department to make fencing materials: we could therefore be more usefully employed trying to ensure we didn't need to chip on dry days. Our view was that spending a day sweating like pigs in debris covered waterproofs was far better than staying dry while bathing in creosote fumes. Unfortunately, even in the depths of winter this didn't entirely obviate the necessity of spending some Fridays there.

CHAPTER 16
PLANTING AND FENCING

Erecting a rabbit proof netting fence round Stoney Field was to be our next job in 1979. Situated north east of Hooksway it was as the name implied a field and the soil contained a great many flints: these made it very hard on plough shares. For one reason or another a decision had been made to plant it with trees: I believe this had more to do with its inability to produce good crops and deer damage than worn shares but wasn't party to the discussions which decided its future. The name gave us little confidence that it would be an easy job, though we were able to borrow a tractor mounted post driver from the farms department to hammer in the seven foot strainers which would save many hours of hand digging and ramming. I asked Kevin to get it and set off while Tim, Phil and I put a chainsaw, crowbar, spades, a rammer, drivall, half a dozen rolls of rabbit netting, plain wire and staples in the Land-Rover before driving to the pickle yard, Mike taking one of our tractors and a trailer to load with stakes, strainers and struts. That done we made our way to Stoney Field, arriving soon after Kevin and waiting a few minutes for Mike before having lunch at nine o'clock: as he had all the woodwork we could not start in any case.

The field was entirely surrounded by woodland, either plantations or natural regeneration, which had long ago become established on previously open downland. Trying to put posts in close to large trees usually presents problems because of the number of roots they have to penetrate, but here we had sufficient leeway to avoid most of them without encroaching far into the field, though we could not avoid the stones. We walked all round the edge deciding where best to put the strainers, Mike driving slowly alongside so we could take one off the trailer approximately every hundred yards: the plain wire was not high tensile and long runs were difficult to strain effectively with our big 'dogs', a tool which looked like a pair of very large, long handled nut crackers. There was to be a wide ride diagonally across the new plantation connecting with those in the adjoining woods and this determined where the gateways were to be created: we marked this out with two lines of short sticks. The field sloped very slightly and we began work at a lower corner where one of the gates had to be. While Kevin and Tim used the tractor and post driver to hammer in two strainers to create the gateway, the regular loud echoing clonks of heavy steel on wood announcing to the world what was happening, Phil and I began setting out stakes along the intended line from the first, one every three paces. As soon as they had the gateway established they worked their way along the field, hammering in further strainers. This had to be done as quickly as possible because the farms wanted their post driver back as soon as we could finish with it, preferably yesterday: we would therefore have to put the stakes in by hand with a heavy drivall.

To ensure a straight line between the strainers we rolled out part of a coil of plain wire, strained it just enough to remove any curves and stapled it loosely to them, close to the ground making sure it was on their outward sides. I then started crowbarring holes along the inside of the line, Phil standing a stake in each, and we quickly established a routine of twelves, driving these in before making further holes to give ourselves frequent breaks from the heavy drivall. We did the first hundred yards, making sure the first and last stakes were less than three paces from the strainers so they could act as stops for the lower end of the struts which were eight feet long and required to brace the strainers: without these the tension of the wire would gradually pull them over. I cut a notch in each strainer with the chainsaw then trimmed the top of the struts to match, knocked them into place and hammered a six inch nail through each to make sure they couldn't move. Now we could begin wiring.

The plain wire had to be tight and three feet from the ground because its purpose was to support the top of the netting: we began by fixing it firmly to the gatepost strainer then tensioning it onto the one at the end of our line of stakes, gripping it in the jaws of the dogs and levering round the post until it was as tight as we could get it before stapling it into place. Rather than put in a further run of stakes I decided to complete the section by putting up the netting, firstly digging a shallow trench the width of our spades along the outer edge of the line of stakes to take the turned out bottom of the netting: the amount of stones we hit in the process suggesting whoever was to plant the field would not have an easy job. Laying the bottom six inches outward then replacing the excavated soil greatly reduced the likelihood of rabbits getting underneath as they usually started digging at the foot of vertical netting. Unclipping the first we laid the drivall on its loose end and unrolled it along the line until we reached its last few feet. I asked Phil to hold it while I got the second roll so we could join them together on the ground: only by doing so could we ensure the top would continue in a straight line and gloves were essential to avoid spiking our fingers as we twisted the cut ends. A mistake here would become obvious the moment we tried to tension the second roll onto the stakes, as would having the wire the wrong way up. Rabbit netting has a top and bottom, not easily discernable by eye and rolls were marked with small tags on their top edge when manufactured to avoid users putting it upside down. The reason for this is that the top edge is pre-tensioned but the bottom can be stretched a bit, enabling it to be moulded over small irregularities and into shallow depressions: put the wrong way up it could not be pulled tight and looked awful, sagging away from the plain wire to which it had to be fixed. We stapled the end onto the first strainer then I tensioned it up to the plain wire at each stake in turn by putting my fingers through several holes and pulling it as taut as I could while Phil put in a staple. Mike followed on, stapling the now vertical netting onto the stakes and we finished by fixing it to the plain wire with twists of fine wire in three places between them. To make sure the loose bottom edge laid flat in the trench we creased it carefully with our spades before raking the excavated earth over it and treading it into place.

We completed the section before I glanced at my watch to discover it was dinnertime. I shouted to Tim and waved my arms but it took a few moments to attract his attention: Kevin in the tractor could hear nothing but the engine and banging of the post driver but quickly got the message when Tim made glass lifting gestures to him. The noise ceased abruptly and they walked down to join us in the Land-Rover for a bite to eat, our sandwiches spiced with a generous helping of jollity. No matter how unpleasant the job, and this was by no means a bad one, humour always helped progress and never failed to emerge when we were together: it also seemed to speed the dinnertime break and all too soon I had to suggest it was time to start again.

Having put in a further run of stakes we stood for a few moments admiring our handiwork then saw Tim approaching: he brought depressing news. They had reached the top of the field and found the post driver was unable to knock in the strainers there. I walked back with him for a look at the problem and a few moments spadework discovered the reason: there were barely eight inches of soil above the solid chalk. Ploughing, coupled with the effect of rain had over many years, gradually moved a lot of it downhill: this meant we would have to hand dig holes here and the job would take longer than planned. I asked them to go back to the bottom and work round the other way until they met the same problem: the post driver could then be returned to the farms and we would know how many strainers we had to dig in.

I was very pleased with our rate of progress: Tim and Kevin joined us when they had put in all the strainers except the few along the top edge and in a week we had completed all but this section. Digging in these last few wasn't as hard as I feared; the chalk bedrock broke up easily when hit with the crowbar and packed in very firmly around them when rammed down. With this side finished all that remained was to make lift off gates using some 4"x2" rails brought from the pickle yard, stapling netting across their frames and we could then 'shut the doors'. Deer would still get over the fence but we didn't think any rabbits were trapped inside. The field was ready for planting during the coming winter.

In February 1980 Ian told us we were to do the planting, probably with some help from one of the other gangs for the first couple of days. We were timber felling in Bruton Wood at the time and this had dragged on for weeks: it was a job I was getting a little tired of and to have a complete break from the confines of helmet and earmuffs, the whine of chainsaws, holdups due to the weather and all too frequent breakdowns of the Skidder was extremely welcome. To cap it all, partway through Ian had increased the parcel from 20,000 to 30,000 cube as the buyer was paying a good price and wanted as much as he could get.

The trees for all the winter planting had been supplied bare rooted as usual, tied in bundles of fifty and on delivery were stored inside a temporary rabbit proof enclosure at the end of a small field separated from the village by the disused railway embankment: it had once been the estate nursery. The bundles were heeled in to keep their roots moist and protected from wind and frost until they were required. We dug out what I estimated would be sufficient bundles to last us the day – beech, Norway maple and thuja (western red cedar), the three species we had to plant – and put them straight into plastic sacks, covering them with our planting bags and spades in the back of the Land-Rovers to prevent them becoming dry during the run out to Stoney Field. The tiny root hairs through which a tree absorbs water and nutrients could be killed by a few seconds exposure to a breeze and new ones could take two weeks to grow: the tree itself could die if the entire root was dried off so we took great care of them. Even now I want to shout when I see folk throwing little trees on the ground or waving them about before planting. Our vehicle was a long wheelbase and we also put in a bundle of tall sticks for marking out our planting lines.

With Chris and Adam joining us at least for the first two days we hoped to make rapid progress. Kevin and I had our shotguns and having walked the new fenceline looking for holes – it was not unheard of for badgers or rabbits to dig under the lightly buried bottom of the netting before it became firmly anchored by grass roots – we walked back and forth across the field in a line hoping to flush any rabbits or hares which had been fenced in. Not one did we see, though there were several 'forms', the lying up places made by hares in the grass and scatters of deer droppings: a three foot fence would not keep them out.

Except in some ornamental work we always planted trees in straight rows because it made thinning and timber extraction much easier when they grew to marketable size: these had to be put in as near 90 degrees to the central ride as we could make them. To get this alignment we began by setting out a line of marking sticks six feet apart along the edge of the ride in the centre of the field, one for each of us. Chris then picked up an armful and set off more or less at a right angle to this line, stopping a short distance from the fence and looking back for directions. I waved him a few yards to the left and he tried to push one stick into the ground, but it fell over. Anticipating we might have some difficulty with this I had put a crowbar in our Land-Rover before leaving the yard: Kevin took it over to him and together they put in the line, parallel with those along the ride edge and also six feet apart. Adam and Phil each picked up six sticks and walked towards them, one stopping halfway and the other when only a few yards short. I stepped back across the ride and lined up the near and far left hand sticks while Adam held one of his upright and looked back at me. Directing him with hand signals and shouts of left a bit, right a bit I was able to position it in a direct line with the other two then repeated the procedure with Phil. Lining up the rest was done in a similar way, Kevin crowbarring small holes when required, and finally we each had four sticks to sight along, ensuring as far as possible the planted trees would be in straight lines, though there was always a little 'wandering' when planting and some wandered more than others, occasionally even crossing into the adjoining row! These very wayward trees had to be dug out and replanted, the offender receiving a good deal of ribald verbal abuse while he did so.

Our instructions were to plant in pure rows – beech, thuja, Norway, thuja, beech, thuja and so on, the faster growing conifers acting as a nurse crop to draw the hardwoods up straight. It had not escaped anyone's notice that the thuja roots were shorter and more pliable than either of the others and there was a minor dash to grab bundles of these. To avoid a good natured mêlée I asked Chris, Adam and Kevin to plant them for our first rows while the rest of us took the hardwoods and we would change over after each row to ensure fairness. I chose beech and put two bundles in my bag, cutting their strings before letting the large flap on the bag flop over the open top to protect the little trees: at six foot spacing in the rows this was sufficient to cover two hundred yards which I reckoned would be plenty for these longest rows: we didn't bother to step out the distance to the fence. Stoney Field was well named: the first stab with my spade struck a flint barely under the surface and went no further. Shifting my point of aim slightly a second attempt found softer ground, the blade sinking to half its depth. I trod on the step and levered back and forth, the blade grating against more hidden flints to create a slot deep and wide enough to take the roots without screwing them up, a big planting sin. Pulling a tree from my bag I held the slot open with the spade and slipped its roots down alongside, making sure it was at the same depth it had grown in the nursery, withdrew the spade, held the little tree upright then thumped the ground all around it with my heel to ensure no air was trapped and it was firmly held. Planting too deep or not deep enough could kill them due to rotting of the stem or root exposure. Everyone was experiencing equal difficulty making holes deep enough and our initial progress was very slow.

Planting is a satisfying occupation, even more so when the soil is deep and moist. Away from the top edge of the field it may well have qualified on both counts, but soft it most definitely was not, the amount of stone making it the geological equivalent of a heavily fruited Christmas cake. The clash of steel on flint became a regular and frequent sound, occasionally producing dull red sparks, the shocks jarring wrists and more than once a voice was raised in four letter frustration at the impossibility of making a hole in the right place: a little wandering here would have to be accepted by the forester, between the rows and within them or the field would never be planted. We bashed our way slowly on, now and then having to use the crowbar to make a decent hole because it proved impossible to penetrate the stones with our spades: no wonder the farmer gave it up!

As foreman it was my responsibility to ensure the job was done properly: several times during the day I walked over to a row, gripped a tree between my forefinger and thumb, giving it a gentle tug to check it was firm. One pulled out and I quickly replanted it before checking those either side in the same row. They were well anchored but I mentioned it loudly enough that everyone heard and I hoped took note: had they all been loose the offender would have been called back to do a better job. I imagine foresters had been doing a similar thing for generations: Arthur, Jack and Frank all did. Well planted and with sufficient moisture the little trees' growing roots would easily push down between the abundant stones, far more easily than brute force blows from steel spades, enabling them to absorb water and nutrients and provide firm anchorage to resist the push of strong winds: in twenty years deer, rodents and weather permitting Stoney Field would become a young wood. A commemorative tree, planted in an open space is there for all to see: most of our plantings would never be so obvious to many people and bear no brass plaques, but in years to come we would be able to see the results of our labours, here and elsewhere across the estate: we signed our names on the soil with growing wood and that, for me at least, is a source of great pride.

It was pure coincidence that while writing this chapter I was given a photocopy of a letter written in 1908 by a recently retired forester describing the condition of the estate woodlands in the 1890s at the time it was purchased by William James. He mentioned a dramatic increase in the price of beech timber between 1898 and 1902 because the Government was buying large quantities "chiefly, most of the time, for making tent pegs for our troops in South Africa." That was the Boer War of 1899–1902. The estate had taken advantage of this situation by bringing forward some of its felling plans and 515 trees were cut in Buriton Hanger (it was known as Buriton Wood in those days), the plantation bounding the west side of Stoney Field. The beeches were almost certainly planted after this felling: they were the right age, about eighty years old, a thought which brings history closer. As to whether any members of my family were involved in the felling or replanting I do not know; there were certainly Boxalls working on the estate at that time and it is quite possible one of my ancestors left his signature in the trees I could see beyond the rabbit netting fence.

———•———

It remained bright and fairly sunny but rather blustery all morning, making it essential our trees were kept covered in the planting bags which some, including me, carried over one shoulder, others laid on the ground: providing they weren't left open for the wind to get in it really didn't matter which method was preferred. Unfortunately the broken cumulus clouds began to coalesce during our dinner break and take on a look of imminent rain, a cool dampness replacing the warmth of the morning hours, but the weather gods decide to look kindly on us, allowing a full, uninterrupted day's work and by hometime to everyone's surprise we had planted a considerable area: weather permitting we would be back on Monday for a second bash.

One or more of our number must have upset a higher authority over the weekend because low grey, scudding cloud and a stiff south westerly wind greeted us Monday morning, giving every indication that we should not expect divine intervention a second time. Spatters of drizzle began falling as we set about completing the partly planted rows left on Friday, managing only to finish them and set out the lining sticks for the next rows before the spattering became opaque grey sheets drifting across the field, forcing us at least temporarily to take cover in the vehicles. The heavens were unhappy, as were we: deer and the so far invisible hares had enjoyed the weekend checking out our planting and appeared to have a particular liking for the Norway maples as quite a few were minus their terminal buds, some half eaten! Deer have no upper incisors and their bites left a ragged edge whereas those bitten through by hares were snipped off cleanly and some of the decapitated tops, stripped of buds, lay beside the small stumps of the trees. It was very depressing to find so much damage done so quickly: the estate deer stalker would have to pay the field serious attention and we needed to scour it thoroughly in search of the hare or hares: it was unlikely all to have been the work of one very greedy individual with the appetite of a labrador.

While we enjoyed a slightly early drinktime the drizzle turned to rain, pattering heavily on the roof, and left us in no doubt it had set in for the rest of the day. There was no point getting soaked and in any case, when the ground became really wet it was more inclined to stick to our boots than tread down nicely around the trees, making it more difficult to plant properly. We returned to West Dean and I spent the rest of the day in the workshop – having taken the others to the pickle yard – sorting through our collection of old and broken chainsaws, repairing two which Ian wanted to sell.

Frost and having to attend a first aid course in the college kept us away until Thursday, though the other gang managed to get more planting done on Tuesday when Phillip shot a hare. We made another search of the field before starting, but found no more: maybe there really was only the one and it possessed a prodigious appetite. Pigeons were flying over way out of range and to satisfy our desire for a few shots we contented ourselves with firing at, and missing, a hand thrown polythene, dinner plate sized Frisbee which had somehow found its way into our Land-Rover: as our shots rang out the pigeons abruptly changed their flightline, passing even further away. Fun over, we got down to the serious work and by the end of the day had planted almost half the field. I put in a scatter of oak, one here and there to add a little variety and give the plantation greater value to wildlife in the decades to come: to avoid the prospect of missing rows, as the Norway maples were still being hammered by deer, I took an executive decision and changed the hardwood planting to three beech, three Norway within each row. Unsuitable weather and having to go chipping then kept us away for more than a week: as happened with the timber felling, circumstances could conspire to make any of our jobs take far longer than planned and there was to be no exception on this occasion, to the forester's undoubted frustration.

Joe was rustled up to lend a hand when we finally returned: he was pleased to get out of the mill for a day or two and thoroughly enjoyed the planting and rough humour. We made steady progress and fairly quickly covered the second half of the field, thankful that even in the top where the soil was shallow it still possessed enough depth to plant in, though the trees would not be able to put down many deep roots and might in years to come be liable to blow over in very strong winds. Deer continued to make nightly visits to check on our progress and damage more trees, but now there were so many the effects of their nibbling became greatly diluted; however, the stalker would still be expected to cull some of the interlopers and thus persuade the rest it was not a healthy place to visit. The huge cost of deer fencing could not be justified so to a degree the little trees had to take their chances, but enough would grow to create a plantation, even many of those badly chewed would 'get away' given time.

CHAPTER 17

FELLING MEMORIES

Each year felling trees was a major part of our work, particularly through the winter months and during my time in the Woods Department I cut tens of thousands, from saplings to ancient leviathans. It is impossible to remember them all, but I can still recall a surprisingly large number which remain memorable for a variety of reasons, good and bad.

One young beech, only a foot in diameter at the butt, unexpectedly snapped in half as it fell, the top coming back and flattening me to the ground, knocking off my earmuffs – this was prior to the arrival of safety helmets – and putting the saw out of tune. Jack and Ian shouted a warning and I could see what was about to happen but had time only to shield my head with one arm before it hit me, luckily hurting little more than my pride. The break point was almost completely dead and brittle, the result of fungal attack where a patch of bark had been stripped some years previously by squirrels. On a Saturday morning something struck me in the mouth while trimming out a felled tree: to this day I have no idea what, but it meant a trip to hospital for some stitches in my lower lip which had unintentionally acted as a shock absorber between the object and my front teeth. The following week I was subjected to a considerable amount of micky taking by the other young woodies as a result, mostly deliberately slurred speech while grinning and holding their lower lips down at angles in greatly exaggerated imitation of my swollen one.

I felled a very tall beech shaped like an enormous bean stick which had only a small tuft of branches at the top and discovered, in a slit sixty feet from its butt end, two dead, ringed bats: these I was able to identify with the aid of a book I took the following day as mouse eared, our largest species. Having sent the rings to the London Zoo address stamped on them and subsequently received a visit from Dr Bob Stebbings, the national bat expert, I learned the sad news that I could now claim to have killed the last known female in Britain! On a more positive note, he told me the accident had supplied some new information about their way of life. No-one knew where they roosted in summer and droppings collected from the hole allowed him to identify prey remains as being from ground living beetles, indicating that they fed either on the ground or picked their prey from it. As there were apparently no more females, knowing this seemed to be rather academic as the species would become extinct in a few years unless there were others as yet undiscovered or numbers were augmented by immigration from the continent.

In no way intended to be a punishment for the unfortunate mishap, he persuaded me to carry out a survey of buildings across the area to see if I could find any more: it was obviously impossible to search two thousand acres of trees for roost sites. With Charlotte I visited a lot of houses on the estate and others close by, discovering many colonies of several species, but no more mouse eared: one large house had no less than five species which came and went through holes in its somewhat dilapidated roof. We were also invited to go with him on his annual winter visit to some old railway tunnels where the unfortunate mouse eared and many other bats hibernated and where they had been ringed. The work got us on local radio and in the papers but didn't kindle a desire to spend my future studying them; I did however learn a great deal about the much maligned and misunderstood little mammals.

Dutch elm disease reared its ugly head across much of the south in the 1970s and those on the estate did not escape its ravages: the largest trees were a characteristic part of the farmland scene at that time and they began to die. Attempts were made to save some of the most conspicuous by injecting them with fungicide, but this resulted in nothing more than dead strips running upward from the small holes bored to introduce the chemical. It was decided, reluctantly, to fell them and in a further unsuccessful attempt to halt the spread of the disease most were burned.

We felled one between Preston Farm and Binderton and were under instructions to burn every part of it: to me this seemed a terrible waste of good timber, but orders were orders. Having trimmed it out all the dead twiggery and cordwood were piled along and on top of the great butt from which the bark had begun peeling, though the timber itself was still sound and sappy. We put several old tyres among the wood, poured gallons of diesel and waste oil along it and sprinkled chainsaw petrol in several places before throwing a lighted, petrol soaked rag on one end and standing back to watch the conflagration develop. Sheets of angry red flame crept along the heap as the diesel and oil ignited, forcing us back. The column of thick black smoke grew ever larger as wood and tyres began to burn, the immense heat warming the side of the Land-Rover which had been parked well away, reddening our faces and driving the smoke vertically for some way before the breeze was able to overcome its resistance and carry it away. I was sure from a distance it could easily have been mistaken for an aircrash and was very relieved not to hear the wail of approaching sirens, though we had taken the precaution of warning local residents what was going to happen. There was nothing more we could do but come back in the morning to poke in the ends and pick up the steel wires remaining from the tyres so they would not be a hazard to the farm's dairy cattle: being inquisitive by nature they would certainly investigate the area thoroughly.

One of the Binderton residents told us when we returned that the fire had blazed for hours, well into the night, therefore it was no surprise to find few ends to poke in: all the cordwood and tyres had been reduced to a huge halo of still smoking grey ash in which the butt, black all over sat virtually unharmed by the prolonged roasting it had been subjected to! Having radioed Frank and informed him of our unhappy discovery he told us to cut it into logs and distribute loads around the estate to those wanting firewood. As it was entirely covered with a crust of charcoal, reducing it to manageable chunks with saws and axes was a very long and extremely dirty job which made us and our equipment filthy: we rapidly acquired the appearance of Victorian chimney sweeps, with boots and the bottoms of our jeans covered in the pale grey ash and for a time our usual sense of humour entirely deserted us. It proved impossible, however, not to smile at the thought that those unlucky enough to be the recipients of this largesse would hardly greet it with pleasure, a fate which befell at least one trustee. The wood warmed us twice and those who received what amounted to a load of large blocks could also expect to gain two warms and require a good bath as the lumps needed to be further reduced in size before they would fit into a woodburner or on an ordinary open fire, a muscle building task in itself as one of the characteristics of elm is its reluctance to split. As the butt was almost entirely green and sap filled they would also have to wait a few years for the logs to season before they would burn, as we had already discovered.

To the watcher, felling a tree appears a simple task; cut out the sink to aim it then make the back cut and over it goes. However, appearances can be deceptive and rarely is it this easy. It was vitally important to 'read' a tree, particularly a large one, and normal practice to walk round it looking for any lean, signs of butt rot or stones trapped in the claws which would effect how it could be felled and check the wind direction before standing back against the trunk and looking along the intended line of fall for any obstacles or other potential problems: only then would we start the saw. On Battens Hanger, where we were clear felling an area of beech, I came to one shaped like a huge catapult with a slight amount of lean: it wanted to fall one stem above the other which would guarantee a split butt as the top limb would whip down with enormous force when the lower one struck the ground. The steep slope also had to be taken into consideration. To avoid wasting good timber and losing piecework money we tried whenever possible to put such trees down flat, ensuring both limbs struck at the same time. Sizing up this particular situation I cut it to fall slightly at an angle to the place I wanted it down so it would brush against another tree, causing it to roll and fall flat. Often the ploy works, though on this occasion it didn't. It fell exactly as I intended, slid off the other tree but failed to rotate by even one degree and with a loud crack the butt split from end to end as the top limb smacked down. From further up the slope came a variety of rude comments as it was now suitable only for firewood.

Felling Cemetery Rew in West Dean was an unusual job: a number of mature beech showing signs of disease had to be removed. It was not possible to drop them into the cemetery and the only other option was to fell them across the main road. My gang looked forward to this because we would be able to stop the traffic and even better, one of the other gangs would be doing the clearing up when we had dragged them clear of the carriageway, up the bank into a field on the opposite side. I viewed the job with a degree of sadness because the trees supported a long established rookery and as a boy, when my family lived at number 101 by the river, I watched their comings and goings every day and always enjoyed hearing them about.

The police, council and local radio were duly contacted and we were informed that blocking the road for up to twenty minutes at a time did not require any of the boys in blue to be present: this meant each tree could be felled, cut up as necessary before being winched clear, the tarmac swept clean of twiggery and the accumulated traffic allowed to proceed on its interrupted way while we made ready to cut the next. It did not take long to discover twenty minutes was a very short window and we could not afford to loiter when each tree was down. The younger members of the gang took perverse pleasure in seeing how many buses we could hold up each time though their drivers, with schedules to keep, appeared far from amused to judge from the scowls we were treated to as they passed. A policeman did come by once to see how we were getting on and his arrival was fortuitous: as I stood talking to him a car suddenly arrived beside us, having jumped the queue and ignored the stop sign. I think the driver had cause to regret his impatience.

Using a winch to pull trees against their lean, or which for a variety of other reasons could not be wedged over, was a necessity and on many occasions made tricky jobs comparatively easy to do without collateral damage to buildings, fences, our vehicles and more importantly ourselves. Very occasionally, however, even this invaluable mechanical assistance required help. One of the great elms in West Dean Park close to the river had to be felled: in order to prevent it going the wrong way a sling was put up it and as winch tractor driver that day I had the job of pulling it over. The tractor had to be positioned beside the river. I took up the strain and put on the ratchet brake when the rope became taut, its rear wheels lifting as the large anchors bit firmly into the earth almost on the edge of the riverbank. Ian cut the tree and I began pulling, but instead of the elm coming over the tractor began dragging backwards, one anchor spade tearing the turf away from the lip of the bank: to operate the winch I was standing on the footplate, facing backwards on that side and viewed with some alarm the imminent prospect of a very unpleasant dip so stopped pulling. It was obvious that to continue would result in the tractor rolling into the river with me in all probability under it rather than the tree falling. To get out of what had become a very tricky situation one of the other tractors was brought up and chained to it, but until the elm was falling under its own weight I remained somewhat nervous and confess to breathing a deep sigh of relief when it hit the ground.

I can only remember one occasion when it became necessary to give serious human help to a winch. In the park again several years later I had to fell a beech which, because it had grown in the open, was cauliflower shaped and had a slight lean over a recently fenced and planted area. It had to be winched directly against its lean to ensure this new planting wasn't damaged if it fell slightly off the point of aim. The beloved old Massey Ferguson winch tractor had recently been sold and we were entirely reliant on the Skidder for pulling power, but winching over large trees was not something it had been designed to do. It had no anchors to provide the necessary firm grip, only the tread on its four big tyres and its winches were mounted higher than the rear axle: heavy pulling above their height tended to lift the rear end slightly, further reducing its grip. Well aware of this shortcoming and as far as possible to overcome it we put a sling up the tree as usual and attached both winch ropes to it for extra pulling power before I began cutting. There were no flints hidden among the claws and the saw, newly sharpened sliced through the wood like a razor. Having completed the felling cut I stepped away several paces to be well clear of the butt in case it kicked back and signalled Mike to begin pulling. The tree shook slightly but never moved, the Skidder merely dragging itself backwards and sliding down the slope. He stopped winching, let the ropes go slack to reposition it then tried again with the same result. To win some extra grip he left the winch brakes on and spun the wheels in forward gear, each swiftly digging a hole in the ground, but additional attempts resulted only in further gentle shaking of the tree and the tractor dragging partly out of its newly created holes. He finally admitted defeat when one of the winch ropes snapped.

There was now only one option: we had no second tractor to chain to it so the sling would have to be moved higher up the tree. Mike slackened off the remaining rope while Kevin and I put the ladder back against the tree and began to climb for the second time, all too well aware that our safety depended entirely on the strength of the hinge of uncut wood and very grateful there was little wind. While Kevin took the weight of the sling and winch rope I undid the shackle and together we clambered further up the tree, dragging their combined weight with us, reattaching the sling as high as we could get it. Failure now would mean having to cut through the hold, a dangerous task in itself as the tree would probably fall backwards and I would have to run out beneath a mass of rapidly descending large limbs: I quickly dismissed this as being a measure of very last resort. It would also be acutely embarrassing if it did go backwards as it would demolish a sizeable area of young trees and rabbit proof fence. We returned to earth much relieved, brought down the ladder and carried it beyond reach of the tree, whichever way it eventually fell, before waving to Mike. He started the Skidder and began pulling, having still to make several attempts with the single rope before the tree eventually began to lift, reached its point of balance and fell, striking the earth with a long, splintering crash which echoed down the park and must have awakened anyone having an afternoon nap in the college. The dust was still settling when over the brow appeared Ian's Land-Rover: he had with him a health and safety inspector! This incident, and a number of other annoying but less potentially dangerous ones resulting from having to use the Skidder in this manner led to the purchase of a good line pulling winch with anchors which could be attached to a tractor's three point linkage.

In Calhouns plantation, which we clear felled in stages over several years, I trimmed out a nice straight beech which had been felled along the slope. To do this safely I began by going along the lower side, sawing off the limbs, cutting them into cordwood lengths and stacking up before working my way around the head of the tree and back along the top side, becoming increasingly surprised it showed no tendency to roll as I cut off the last few limbs. I had already warned those working below to move away from the danger zone because of what I expected was about to happen. Moving a few pieces of lop to create enough open space I stacked the last of the cordwood then went to the butt end and looked along its lower side, expecting to see something trapped under it and acting as a support. There was nothing obvious so I walked along its top side, leaning over as far as I dared for a closer look. A small twig, no thicker than my little finger was all I could see still attached to the tree, its broken end pushed into the ground: there were no large lumps of wood or anything else which could possibly be restraining it. Picking up my saw and drop starting it I leaned over the butt again and touched the twig with the tip of the bar, firmly believing this tiny thing could not be holding up several tons of wood. Instantly it parted and the butt rolled, brushing the saw aside, colliding with, rolling over and scattering the lower heap of cordwood before stopping with a loud clonk against two butts several yards further down the slope. David and Jack walked back to work on their trees as I explained what had caused the problem and set about restacking the spread of cordwood, having to prise a couple of pieces from the soft ground into which its great weight had pushed them.

It was here we also had a narrow escape from a widowmaker. Several of us were working on a tree which had fallen into a tangle of growth amid several other standing trees when, for a reason no-one could explain Jack suggested we stop and have an early lunch. It was most unusual. As we made our way to the Land-Rover a loud crack and moments later an equally loud crash made us look back: a large ash limb a foot in diameter had fallen from one of the surrounding trees and was laid across the one we had been working on seconds earlier. It had obviously been weakened by our tree as it fell and had given way. To this day I wonder if some kind of sixth sense had warned Jack of the danger or if it was simply luck: whichever, there is no doubt one or more of us would have been seriously hurt or killed had we still been there.

On occasion the most unorthodox methods were required to get a tree down in the right place: one in particular, a dead elm in a rew near the White Horse pub in Chilgrove sticks in my memory. It was not very large but leaned heavily over the lane, known rather inappropriately in such a rural location as the High Street, and had been forced to grow that way in search of light by a much larger sycamore which was growing directly behind. It could not be felled into the lane because of an iron fence which bordered the rew, or winched over against its lean because the sycamore was to be retained. After a little head scratching I decided on what I hoped would be a painless solution to the dilemma: we put one of the Skidder's winch ropes over a limb on the sycamore and attached it to the smaller tree then tied a long hemp rope to it as well. I cut the tree as if it was to be felled towards the sycamore, enabling Mike to pull it upright and hold it there while I put in a second sink a foot higher and at a right angle to the first. The rest of the gang took hold of the hemp rope and stood as far away as possible, facing this sink and after making the second felling cut I joined them. Signalling to Mike to let his rope out slowly we pulled on ours to keep pace and bring the tree down towards us. To my delight the plan worked perfectly and it came to rest harmlessly in the rew.

The author felling a big lime

The photo, taken in 1979, shows me stepping back to watch the fall of a great lime I had just cut at Great Combes. This tree proved to be 130 feet tall and produced 440 hoppus feet of timber: I remember it particularly not for its size – I have felled much larger trees – but for what purpose its soft white wood was destined. Beer barrel bungs! Understandably the bung makers demanded timber as clean and knot free as possible: this great butt and its lesser companions were considered ideal material and fetched the estate a very good price, though as someone whose intake of alcoholic liquors would swiftly have reduced any pub to bankruptcy it seemed a rather ignominious end for such fine trees.

Our sense of humour could at best be described as robust, possibly rough, and gave little quarter, but timber felling can be extremely dangerous and there was no larking about when we were dealing with tons of wood which had the potential to kill us or those we were working with. Knowing when to pull legs and play the fool harmlessly was a vitally important part of the job and it says much for the department that minor accidents were rare and no serious ones ever occurred.

CHAPTER 18
THE OPEN AIR MUSEUM

In September1970, the year I joined the Woods Department, at the northern end of the estate the newly formed Weald and Downland Open Air Museum opened its gates to the public for the first time. Sited in an idyllic spot by the junction of the A286 and the small lane which ascends Singleton Hill on forty acres of pasture and woodland leased from the estate, we were able to watch its development over the years from a sparse scatter of old buildings, rescued from many parts of southern England into one of the country's most important collections of our building heritage. Not only did we watch, we worked there many times, felling and clearing trees as the museum expanded to make more room for car parking, office and building space, removing dangerous trees and clearing up the occasional windblows. For several years I was mentioned by name and seen in a photo on one of their information boards! I always enjoyed working there because it gave me the opportunity to have a look round free of charge during our dinner breaks and view the latest exhibits, be they buildings or old tools. I felt a bond with the many men, now dust, their names lost, whose craftsmanship over the centuries shaped the beautiful timbers and cut the intricate joints visible in every building and which, thanks to the work of the museum, had been saved from the match.

In December 1973 I drove the winch tractor into the huge white excavation which was shortly to become the lake and set it up to pull over two diseased beeches overhanging the main road. There was some urgency to get the job done because the lining and filling was scheduled to begin in the New Year. We had the police in attendance to stop the traffic in case anything fell in the road and burned all the lop on the pristine chalky lake bed. As it was to be clay lined our running about and the fire site caused no problems, though we took care to remove every bit of twiggery we could sensibly rake up. Jack, Ian, Mike and I were there again the following December, cutting a number of trees on an area to be bulldozed and turned into a car park when we were invited to join the staff for a pre-Christmas drink in Bayleaf, their 15th century farmhouse saved from destruction in Chiddingstone, Kent. At dinnertime we went in to find them all sitting on low wooden benches around a coke fire blazing warmly on the original stone hearth in the central hall. A bench was brought for us, everyone shuffled round a bit to make space for it and we were plied with cider and Christmas cake, staying there happily for the rest of the afternoon while a column of heat shimmered above the fire and dispersed among the rafters for the hall was open to the roof, a characteristic feature of such medieval buildings, as was the absence of glass in the windows which allowed the cold December air to creep in behind us. We learned later that when the cleared area was bulldozed a lot of buried seed had been uncovered, some of which was sent away for identification and proved to be a variety of turnip commonly planted a century earlier! Why this should have been tipped away in the wood will forever remain an intriguing, unsolvable mystery.

At the beginning of April 1981 the news was sprung on us that Ian had been asked if we could put on a two day demonstration of forestry activities there in May, which would involve most of the department. I didn't mind having to do this, but the several football fans among our number were most put out to find Cup Final day was the same weekend and they grumbled so much that the sequence of events we planned were worked in a way which allowed them to get home before kick-off: this greatly reduced but didn't entirely silence the mutterings of disapproval at having to work both days. The intention was to fell several beeches in a clump which had more or less come to the end of its days and would provide an opportunity for us to show visitors the various operations involved in felling and processing timber. The McConnel circular saw was brought from the pickle yard and the chipper towed up specially from its permanent home in the boiler yard. The entire working area was roped off to keep people at a safe distance but allow them close enough to see clearly what we would be doing: it was intended to be entertaining and educational.

As jobs go it was to be an extremely easy weekend: my part in the proceedings being to fell two trees each day, one in the morning and the second early afternoon. Kevin and Keith would trim them out, Mike haul the butts away with the Skidder, Geoff take the branchwood over to the chipper with the forwarder and others to demonstrate it and the circular saw. The only problem from my point of view was that the museum had already planted a replacement group of trees among those to come down, leaving little free space to fell in! There was a distinct possibility some of them and their wire netting guards might get flattened, which would be rather embarrassing for me in such a public demonstration of my ability.

On the Saturday morning a small number of visitors began to gather along the safety rope when I started my saw, attracted by the sound and sight of us moving about, indicating something was about to happen. Among them was Charlotte with Martin, now six months old, in a sling. I'm not sure at that tender age he learned much or absorbed a great deal from being there, but I am very pleased he has chosen to follow my way of life. Perhaps the experience sowed a tiny seed which has subsequently grown and borne fruit. I took more than the usual amount of care in aiming and felling the first tree, Kevin tapping in a wedge to start it falling when I finished the back cut. With an increasing swish of displaced air it fell precisely where I wanted it, between two of the young trees, hitting the ground with a powerful thump and loud crash of breaking branches. A thin ripple of applause came from those watching and the crash attracted a few more passing by to watch the succeeding operations. I put the saw in the Land-Rover and took out the timber tape to measure the butt when it had been headed off before giving a hand to stack the branchwood: Mike and Geoff then came over to move the timber away. Rather than then stand around twiddling my thumbs while the others worked, the circular saw screaming as it cut logs and the chipper grinding loudly through its short feed of branchwood, I went over to the rope and spoke to some of the audience, answering numerous questions and having to explain more than once as folk came up to ask, what we were doing and why. This was actually one of the most enjoyable parts of the day and helped to dispel my own slight fear that visitors would go away thinking we always operated in this one man, one task manner and spent much of our days standing around. The second tree also came down without doing any damage, to slightly louder applause and my great relief, and was dealt with equally efficiently. During our long dinner break we let some of those particularly interested come inside the rope cordon to have a closer look at the equipment and answered still more questions.

At four o'clock when the museum closed we agreed the day had been very successful, but our demonstration was too short so decided to make Sunday's a longer one by felling three trees: there would after all be plenty of time and no cup final to get in the way. When I got home Charlotte told me she had been standing beside a chap who had sucked his teeth and, with a good many loud indrawn breaths been continually critical to his companions of what I was doing – "He's done that wrong" and "I wouldn't have done it like that" were just two of his comments apparently. He may have been more skilled than me or simply airing his ignorance to all those around: I never discovered which and wasn't much concerned in any case, but thought it more likely to have been the latter. Men who really understood how to fell large trees would have made only a few quiet comments to their companions. Those who worked with me and whose opinions I valued considered me to be very good and that was sufficient.

With the show over and the museum staff well pleased we went home very happy with the job so far: two trees remained to be felled and those we did the following week. I confess that one of the tree guards did then get a little buckled: they and the stumps of the trees felled over the weekend combined simply didn't leave enough space for me to completely avoid them. It was very important not to drop a tree onto one of the latter because the resulting shock could easily result in a broken or cracked butt and they were worth a good deal more than the recently planted saplings. To avoid burning any of the grass outside the clump we lit a fire on one of the stumps and Geoff lifted most of the lop onto it with the forwarder, saving us a great deal of heavy dragging.

I have been back to the museum several times over the years since leaving West Dean, to see exhibitions and displays, but my last visit was in search of something more solid than information or memories: I was looking for an axe. The museum keeps a stock of Gransfors Bruks, Swedish axes. I went with my brother-in-law Steve, now a trustee, hoping they had a left handed side axe, but prepared to be disappointed: we left handers are badly catered for in so many things I fully expected to have to order one. The store room was unlocked for us and we went in for a rummage around. It was an axe lover's heaven; hatchets and felling axes, carpenter's axes, log splitters and more were stacked along one side of the almost full room. After a little searching I discovered a pile of side axes and the first one I picked up was left handed! I think of the museum and my days in the woods every time I use it.

Chapter 19
Fire

Fire has served mankind since long before the dawn of history; indeed it is one of our oldest tools, a friend and protector but also on occasions a deadly enemy. We used the most modern equipment in much of our work, inventions our remote ancestors could never have dreamt of, but still relied on this amazing natural process as old as the earth itself to help with many jobs. For me one of the pleasures of being a woodman, though intangible and having no bearing on my ability to do the job was being able to read fires, becoming familiar with the words of books written in the air with inks of scent and sound, together imparting as much information as any printed page about what was being burned, even when the blaze itself could not be seen. Smoke from each species of tree has its own particular scent: that of beech and ash are as different as chalk and cheese, while burning pine possesses a wonderful resiny sweetness quite different from larch. The foliage of yew and other needle leaved trees makes a loud frying sound, like moist chips tipped into boiling fat when thrown onto the flames, holly and rhododendron also, but far more crackly, the result of vapourised sap bursting open their much larger leaves. I have no possible way of discovering if such knowledge gave our remote ancestors any long redundant advantage over their less nasally and aurally aware fellows, but it provided me with another small joy in an occupation I had found all encompassing.

In the depths of winter we started work before daylight and in the early days of 1971 were thinning the rew alongside the main road in the village prior to planting the field between it and Church Clump which covered much of the hill above, this being known as the WI field because of a large wooden hut next to the old bus garage at its eastern end regularly used by the local Women's Institute group. There had been little wind overnight and our fire of the previous day was still alight; a great grey molehill of pale ash, slightly warm to the touch which acted as a blanket, keeping the hot charcoal beneath sealed from the air and preventing it burning away. Snowy raked the top with a stick, revealing glowing coals and a shimmering column of heat filled with sparks and fragments of ash rose into the morning gloaming, appearing to reach all the way to the few stars still shining. It was too dark to begin chainsawing so we raked away more ash, piled on some broken pieces of dead wood and stood around it holding our outstretched hands towards the glorious warmth. A flame licked up through the wood, then more, lighting our faces with their bright yellow glow and illuminating several nearby trees. The heat swiftly increased, becoming too hot to bear and we turned round, almost in unison to toast our backs. All too rapidly these quiet minutes of conversation, contemplation and shared ancient pleasure came to an end: the shadows of night were fast creeping away to their daytime hiding places as a copper and gold stain spread across the south eastern sky, becoming ever brighter as sunrise approached. David started his saw, stripping the fire of its comforting, mystical quality, and we were jolted back to reality.

During my first years in the woods the bodies of chainsaws were made of magnesium alloy, which is both light and very strong. We worked them until they became virtually worn out or suffered mechanical problems. It was uneconomic to repair these cast offs and we put them in the store after stripping them of bars, chains and any other useful parts as the motor units were no longer worth anything. On one occasion we were asked to dispose of five and the simplest way of doing this was to burn them: magnesium, in addition to its other properties, is also flammable at a comparatively low temperature. It was not worth running such a small quantity of metal to the scrapyard in Chichester so we took them down to the sawmill, lit a fire behind the little hut where untold quantities of rubbish had been burned over the years and piled them on top, standing back to eagerly await the light show they would shortly produce. In much earlier years powdered magnesium was used by photographers to create their flashes and it is still a component of white flares. The first one soon began to burn, assisted by the dregs of petrol and oil in its tanks, and a white light as intense as the sun blazed out. This grew and increased still further in brilliance as the others ignited, lighting up the back of the shed and nearby paling fence, overpowering the sun shadows, the sunlight itself on them and impossible to look directly at: they also produced an astounding amount of heat and dense white smoke. We were very impressed with the spectacle, which continued for several minutes before dying as quickly as it started, leaving a circle of white ash lumpy with red hot bearings and crankshafts.

It was a matter of pride to be able to light a fire with one match and no artificial aids, even newspaper: this could be something of a challenge in rainy weather when at first glance nothing dry could be found. There was no point picking up any twigs from the ground because they would be soaking wet and we looked to the standing trees, in particular yew and birch when available because they usually had some dead, small twiggery within reach, the birches often paper thin curls of peeling bark as well which made excellent tinder: in spite of being wet to the touch these aerial twigs remained dry inside and the finest could readily be lit by a match. When time and place permitted I used this method, slowly increasing the size of pieces as the flames gathered strength, shielding their newborn vulnerability from wind if necessary and not permitting anyone to rush the job by putting on large lumps, a guarantee of failure. Some proved unable to do this or simply didn't have the patience, resulting in much wasted time while we stood around waiting in vain for a great heap of branches to burst into flames, but a wisp of wet grey smoke seeping from the top, sometimes with a small hole burned up through the centre like the vent in a volcano, was the usual outcome; what we disparagingly called rooks' nests and were the cause of much ribaldry. These were usually the result of throwing material on higgledy piggledy – as well as too many large pieces – instead of laying it all on more or less the same alignment along the wind until the fire was going really well, the criss-crossed branches making a latticework which was unable to sink down onto the flames. The only reliable remedy for these was to take them apart and start again, wasting more time. Not always was the frontiersman approach possible: sometimes everything was simply too wet and then we resorted to copious newspaper, a pile of twigs and a good dose of chain oil or diesel topped with a generous sprinkling of petrol, ignited with a thrown match: even this approach being known to fail at the first attempt on rare occasions.

Often the wind was useful; a gentle puff helping to get things going and when there was none, if the fire showed a reluctance to burn we used one of our chainsaws as a mechanical bellows, running it at a fast tickover and directing its exhaust at the vital sparks, having made sure the moving chain was clear of any obstacles: this was much easier and more effective than getting down on hands and knees to blow at it or fanning with a sheet of newspaper. Too much however could prove a considerable nuisance as it would blow the flames and virtually all heat out from beneath our carefully built heap, creating a blowlamp effect on the downwind side while much of the wood remained cold. To beat this it was necessary to pile lop on the windward side so it continually fell forward into the fire as its edge exposed to the heat burned away: this had some effect in shielding the fire and prevented it from becoming an elongated sausage shape by the end of a day's work, as it would have done had we thrown wood directly onto the fiercest flames. It was less than fun having to work downwind of such a fire, constantly bathed in smoke and showers of sparks every time more wood was thrown on.

There was little danger, except possibly in some of the younger conifer blocks, that we could inadvertently start a forest fire as there was simply insufficient combustible material in the woods and the same is true for the majority of broadleaved woodland throughout the country. This didn't mean we could afford to be careless, but only once did a fire get out of control and this was entirely the result of the hot dry conditions, not anything we did wrong. We were clear felling part of the beechwood on Battens Hanger and had stopped for dinner, leaving the Skidder parked safely away from the fire, or so we thought. Part way through our sandwiches Kevin said "That smoke is getting closer to the Skidder." We all looked and went on eating, but minutes later realised it was now coming from beneath the tractor and had turned black! Lunch boxes were dropped and we scrambled out of the Land-Rover, running over to it and finding two tyres well alight, oily red flames licking up them and a wide strip of smouldering crushed leaves leading to it from the fire. Using hurriedly grabbed spades and our hands we began throwing dust and dirt on them, successfully extinguishing the blaze, but not before the wall of the front tyre had been burned down to the outer layer of canvas at one point: it had been a narrow squeak. Andy quickly moved it considerably further away, leaving the smell of burned rubber in his wake while we threw more dust over the blackened area to quench what had appeared to be an innocuous creep of tiny flames across the many times driven over, bone dry carpet of beech litter: it gave every appearance of having deliberately sought out the Skidder!

We had many large fires while clearing at Great Combes to dispose of the brambles, lop and top from the trees we felled and abundant dead wood. While we were pulling apart a heap of wet, moss grown poles, the forgotten remains of work many years before and throwing them on our current blaze, a rabbit bolted from beneath them, dodged between our legs and ran straight into the fire. It turned instantly, staggering back with its hair burned black, its eyes greyed dull and sightless by the intense heat and several pairs of hands hurried to grab the first piece of wood they could find with which to bring a swift, merciful end to the unfortunate creatures' terrible suffering. We didn't like what rabbits did to recently planted trees, but had nothing against the animals themselves and felt only great pity for this one; the sudden small tragedy stemming our flow of conversation for several minutes.

On occasions we made use of them for cooking potatoes wrapped in foil and toasting our sandwiches with long forks cut from suitable twigs, Tulip – and we never discovered why he wished to be so called – decided to cook some fish in the same manner one day, putting them at the edge of the fire so they would 'do' slowly and be ready for dinner. Unfortunately he forgot that we were continually throwing more wood on it and by breaktime it had grown considerably: his carefully wrapped fish were now somewhere inside the blaze. Raking about with a prong he eventually located and retrieved the package, the aluminium greyed and in parts bearing evidence of slight melting but faithfully retaining the fish which had been almost entirely reduced to charcoal! We considered his efforts to pick out the remaining edible morsels immensely amusing and laughed uproariously.

Fires in the winter and at other cold times were usually greatly appreciated, but in summer it could be a different story. At Preston Farm a large, bushy macra carpera growing in the narrow space between the garden wall and garage had to be felled: it was brown and dying. On a blazing hot day in July we went down to deal with it, Ian doing the felling while I was on the winch tractor. There was very little space for him to work but the tree came down almost perfectly, its butt bouncing on the wall and as it kicked back, breaking two tiles on the garage roof: we were expecting far more damage. Before we started the trimming out I pulled it clear, the hard, springy limbs taking much of its weight off the wall so no harm came to the brickwork in the process. The others had in the meantime lit a fire and we then began dismembering it. The fire grew as we piled the lop on, the resiny wood burning with ferocious intensity, flames leaping high into the already sweltering summer air and trying their best to reduce us to crisps. Working beside an open furnace could have been no hotter and most shirts, often removed in warm weather to soak up the sun, were kept buttoned to afford us a little protection from the almost skin peeling heat. I thought my first day in the woods, at Blackbush, had been the hottest of my life, but these few hours easily surpassed that solar grilling as we were burned by the sun on one side and the fire on the other with no shred of relief to be had while we worked. Our water bottles were soon drained and we visited the dairy en masse to refill them, spraying each other with the hose as well to cool off: a damp shirt felt extremely refreshing, though dried out in moments on returning to the tree.

The scent of smoke brings back memories of more than flames and heat. It also conjours up the fizzling sound of red hot sparks settling in my hair and occasionally my beard: the smell of burning hair directly under my nose could not be interpreted as someone nearby about to go up in flames and required the most immediate attention. However, fires usually left their mark in the form of holes in our shirts and jackets; a smell of burning fabric indicating the need for a thorough examination of every part we could reach and a call for assistance to beat out smouldering spots on our backs we could not. The scent also stirs memories in some who never spent a day working in the woods: "I remember the smell of woodsmoke and chainsaws," said Jackie the forester's secretary when we met at West Dean many years later. As assistant forester and occasionally before reaching that exalted position I had to go into the office for various reasons and was completely unaware of the heady aroma I took with me. Much cheaper than Chanel or any of the multitude of fragrances available now, it is obviously a powerful combination, though very difficult to put in a bottle.

CHAPTER 20

DEER CULLING AND FAREWELL TO THE WOODS

By the early 1980s a feeling of unrest began to intrude more strongly until it could no longer be ignored. It wasn't simply that specialisation had changed the job and reduced its variety: I had been made assistant forester; had free run of 6000 acres to indulge my interest in conservation, feeling able to make suggestions to the agent about things I considered important for the estate to safeguard, was a member of the West Dean Woods Nature Reserve management committee, warden for the Society of Sussex Downsmen looking after their two small reserves on the crest of the downs, Honorary warden for what had by now become the Nature Conservancy Council at Kingley Vale National Nature Reserve, was married with a wonderful wife and in August 1982 our daughter, Holly, was born: what more could I desire? Boredom was starting to set in, and also disenchantment: I could do the work standing on my head and it was no longer a challenge. I needed something new to exercise my mind as well as my body without taking up almost every waking hour. Early in 1983 something came out of the blue which seemed to provide at least a partial answer, but would make spare time an even rarer commodity.

"The deer culling is being split up, would you be interested in taking some on?" It was a question I was very pleased to answer in the affirmative. I had always enjoyed shooting, mostly with pistols in the days before marriage and children curtailed the large expense and before our pestilential politicians saw fit to deprive me of the right to do so, then with shotguns but had never used a rifle. Numbers of fallow and roe had been increasing for years, in spite of Bob's best efforts working alone in his spare time, the levels of browsing and grazing reaching damaging proportions in places and it had been decided something needed to be done. For a while I heard nothing more on the subject, then Ian told me the stalking was being split into three beats and I would become responsible for the park, arboretum and everything else east of the main road where there were many roe. Initially I would be an apprentice stalker and he would accompany me – he was a member of the local Deer Management Group and already an accredited stalker. Only when he considered me competent, would I be allowed to operate alone and also be eligible to become an accredited stalker with the group. Becoming one of the stalking team would mean I no longer had time during spring and early summer to do my squirrel hopper round and young Mike jumped at the chance to take it on: one evening I drove him round my route, showing him what to do and where to go when the next poisoning season began. The change would mean I lost useful overtime money, but it was a wonderful opportunity handed to me at just the right moment.

In addition to the excitement of anticipation, a considerable part of the pleasure gained from taking up any new activity is choosing the equipment needed to take part in it and I set to work with a will, researching the pros and cons of various rifles suitable for stalking, visiting several gun shops and after the police had processed my Firearms Certificate to allow me to buy one, finally ordering a Ruger .243. Much of my pistol shooting had been with a Ruger revolver and I had a great liking for the brand's understated, traditional styling: they were also far from being the most expensive. While eagerly awaiting its arrival I spent as much time as I could spare creeping around my new beat, binoculars round my neck getting some idea of where deer could be found, alone and with Ian. Stalking as an activity was not new to me: I had spent a great deal of time over the years watching deer and it was treated by some of the woodies as a joke that most autumns I took a week of my holidays during the fallow rutting season to visit Petworth Park and various localities where their wild relations gathered at this time. However, stalking to watch and stalking to shoot are rather different occupations as I was soon to discover.

A few weeks later, when I got home from work Charlotte told me the gun shop had phoned to say the rifle was in. She went to Chichester the following day and withdrew what for us at that time was a very large sum of money to cover its purchase, plus the additional cost of cartridges and a telescopic sight to fit on it. Friday felt a very long day until work finished and I was able to drive to Richard Wells' gunshop in Haslemere, my pocket bulging with the money, returning home with my new acquisition and a quantity of cartridges, feeling as pleased as a dog with two tails. Before taking it out for my first foray it had to be sighted in, to make sure it shot to point of aim. I was able to do the majority of this without firing a cartridge by bore sighting; removing the bolt, laying the rifle upright on a firm support and looking through the barrel at an object – I chose the warning plate on the electricity pole across the common in front of our cottage – then adjusting the telescopic sight so the cross hairs were aligned on the same point.

This task was completed the next evening when I joined Ian and we went to the Withy Beds to check it before going on in search of roebucks. After only four shots and some minor adjustments to the scope it was spot on at a hundred yards, the desired result: my bore sighting had been successful and nothing now stood in the way of me shooting my first deer, or so I naively thought. It was in fact the start of a short but extremely frustrating period: there was no shortage of deer but one opportunity after another passed and I was unable to squeeze the trigger. I was either too slow and the deer wandered off, forgot to release the safety catch, unsteady due to nervous excitement or something obscured the vital parts of the intended target. It is a strange fact that a high velocity bullet will pass through a small tree yet can be deflected by something as slight as a blade of grass, making it of critical importance that there is nothing between the muzzle and target and a safe earth backstop beyond the deer. I could sense Ian's mounting frustration at my apparent inability to break my duck, but was determined not to feel pressured into taking a shot if I wasn't completely happy to do so.

After two weeks of missed chances we were standing in the evening shadows at the edge of Church Clump, looking out over Rough Highdown and the adjoining cornfield when a yearling buck and doe came up out of Warren Hanger, much further away than I considered possible for my first shot at a living deer and in any case there was a barbed wire fence between us. For a while they grazed in the cattle chewed, tussocky grass then slipped through the fence into the lush green corn: it appeared there was to be still more disappointment but moments later, to my surprise the buck turned and began walking slowly along the edge towards us. My heart began pounding like a trip hammer, my body trembled and my mouth suddenly became very dry. Using my tall hazel stave as a support for my front hand and the rifle's forend I looked at him through the scope, realising instantly it would not be possible to shoot using it as a rest because it seemed only to magnify the tremors coursing through me, so I sidestepped carefully to a nearby tree and found its rough barked bole provided a much better, shake free alternative. He continued his meandering but steady progress, nibbling morsels here and there along the narrow unsown edge before pausing, head raised when a cock pheasant suddenly crowed in the hanger, giving me a clear shot at his neck. This was the moment I had waited so long for: I slipped off the safety catch and squeezed the trigger. As the loud boom echoed across the valley he fell sideways through the barbed wire fence and rolled down the lynchet back into Rough Highdown. "They don't come any deader," said Ian with a broad grin on his face, though I doubt it came close to matching mine as we reached the prostrate body and shook hands: my bullet had smashed his spine. Shaking now with a combination of elation and relief I paced out the distance from my firing point – it was seventy five yards – then dragged the buck to a convenient tree and we hung him up so I could perform the gralloch under Ian's watchful eye.

As the culling was to be done in our own time the estate agreed we could keep fifty percent of those we shot to cover at least some of our costs: fuel and ammunition were as now not inconsiderable expenses. This being my first I was determined to keep him to put in our freezer and hung him overnight in the shed at the top of the garden, skinning and butchering him with Charlotte's help the following evening: it took us three hours to complete the task and he produced sufficient venison to keep us in meat for weeks. Over the next few weeks I shot several more with Ian close by before he decided I was sufficiently competent to go out alone, leaving him free to deal with his own beat: I had made no big mistakes and he expressed confidence in my shooting. Only then did I really understand that to be a successful stalker demands total concentration and it is easier to work alone, without a 'shadow', no matter how well meaning and helpful that companion is. I soon learned it was necessary to be entirely at one with my surroundings, to look long, move as slowly and quietly as possible while being aware of everything going on round about. There was no-one following to help, suggest, advise or ensure I did a humane job: I was entirely on my own and must trust myself to maintain high standards. Looking for deer in the woods meant being alert to the flick of an ear, a shadow which didn't quite look right, a tiny sound, the alarm call of a bird; sometimes merely a feeling there was one nearby: being prey animals, constantly alert to danger, cover was very important to them and rarely did they stand broadside in open places as pictures in books usually depict. Spooking deer you are watching can be annoying; doing so when you are trying to shoot one means you have failed in your job and I learned quickly, my previous watching experience having provided a good grounding.

I immersed myself in this new and absorbing activity, gaining confidence and ability as the summer passed, managing successfully to avoid the dangers of becoming over confident because I knew to do so could result in a careless shot or a wounded and lost deer, neither of which I wanted to be responsible for. Charlotte was very supportive, but it became increasingly obvious that I could not continue long term to do so many things. Stalking at dawn and dusk, weekends working at Heyshott Down or the Devil's Jumps for the Downsmen in addition to my full time job meant I was hardly at home during daylight. My state of mind was not helped by learning that the estate was considering cutting some jobs in the department, prompting my search for a full time post in conservation, pursued sporadically and with no great urgency over the past few years to resume in earnest.

There were no jobs advertised which offered me anything like the variety I currently possessed and I had no wish to take something simply in the hope it would get me out of what was developing into a deep rut. The situation had become very strange and not a little depressing: I could not give up my job and lose our tied cottage and didn't want to be forced to choose which of my other activities to finish with, though every day was becoming less pleasurable and I knew something had to change, and quickly. It was amazingly good fortune therefore that one morning in January 1984 I bumped into Mike, an entomologist friend, who asked me if I had applied for the warden's post being advertised by Hampshire and Isle of Wight Naturalists Trust which he thought would be right up my street. This chance meeting, like my decision in 1970 to take up forestry, heralded another momentous change in my life. Far from applying, I hadn't even seen the advert because we didn't read the Guardian, but lost no time in phoning the Trust's HQ for an application form, which I quickly filled in and rushed to the postbox with references and everything else I thought would help only two days before the closing date: the much maligned Royal Mail did its job well, delivering the precious pieces of paper in time. Shortly after I was invited to Romsey for an interview and following this was taken with three more finalists for a brief look at Roydon Woods and Lower Test Marshes, the reserves for which the warden would be responsible. We were then driven back to Romsey and asked to wait outside the interview room for a few minutes before I was called in again and offered the post! I drove back to Hog's Common in something of a daze, told Charlotte the good news and handed in my notice the following morning.

In spite of the excitement I felt great sadness at the prospect of our imminent departure from West Dean and dear old Hog's Common: our small semi detached cottage among the fields was to be exchanged for a dreadful little terraced box surrounded by garish street lights and the railway station in the village of Sway which was the warden's accommodation. My years in the Woods Department gave me an intense feeling of belonging to and being a part of the countryside of my birth and left me with countless memories of times good and bad, of companions now scattered by time and circumstance to the four winds, some regrettably practising their craft in another, greater woodland: all will be remembered as long as I live. The roots which grew so strongly will never be entirely withered or broken: I was born there and no matter how far away I may roam will always retain some of the local chalk in my veins. Machinery has replaced muscle to do many of the tasks I enjoyed: hedge trimming is now carried out by one man on a tractor cocooned in a safety cab, oblivious of the yellowhammer's nest, the glowing hips and haws, wasps and irritating flies; forwarders lift wood far more quickly than hands and the requirement to 'do everything' is fast becoming history. I am proud to be a woodman, to possess the love of working with trees and timber our remote ancestors would have known and to be a member of a sadly diminishing breed.